The Cheapskate's Guide to
WINE

The Cheapskate's Guide to
WINE

How to Enjoy Great Wines at Bargain Prices

Anna Maria Knapp
and Vernon A. Jacobs

Anna Maria Knapp owns Celebrations Wine Club, and
Vernon Jacobs owns Event of the Season Caterers

CITADEL PRESS
Kensington Publishing Corp.
www.kensingtonbooks.com

Dedication
Cheers to Benjamin Franklin, who was the original American
cheapskate. He loved wine as much as he loved a bargain,
realizing that a penny saved was one more penny that
he could spend on wine.

CITADEL PRESS BOOKS are published by

Kensington Publishing Corp.
850 Third Avenue
New York, NY 10022

All Kensington titles, imprints, and distributed lines are available at special quantity discounts for bulk purchases for sales promotions, premiums, fund-raising, educational, or in-
stitutional use. Special book excerpts or customized printings can also be created to fit
specific needs. For details, write or phone the office of the Kensington special sales manager: Kensington Publishing Corp., 850 Third Avenue, New York, NY 10022, attn: Special
Sales Department, phone 1-800-221-2647.

Kensington and the K logo Reg. U.S. Patent and Trademark Office
Citadel Press is a trademark of Kensington Publishing Corp.

First printing: October 2001

10 9 8 7 6 5 4 3 2 1

Printed in the United States of America

Library of Congress Control Number: 2001092630

ISBN 0-8065-2148-1

Contents

Acknowledgments   vii

Introduction   ix

1. Learning About Wines   1
2. Purchasing Wines for Less   13
3. Vintages: Chardonnays, Cabernets, Merlots, and Others Worth Spending Money On   41
4. How Do You Know You Will Like the Wine if You Haven't Tried It?   71
5. Notable Producers Who Consistently Make Outstanding Wines at Outstanding Prices   75
6. Serving Wine   87
7. Collecting Wines   101
8. Insuring and Selling Your Wines   141
9. Auctions   151
10. Restaurants   161
11. I Know Where It's From, but What's in the Bottle?   167
12. Wine and Health   179
13. Past, Present, and Future   183
14. Cheapskate Rules and Regulations   187

Glossary   189

Recommended Books   194

Index   195

Acknowledgments

Wine was part of the beginning of all things when the world as we know it first took shape. Fruit juices that collect in a hollow will naturally ferment into wine without any human intervention. Having said that, we must also acknowledge that the golden nectar that humans first tasted soon oxidized into unpalatable flavors without the intelligence and creativity of drinkers who have labored for millennia to preserve the magical flavors that nature initially delivers.

Although we've known for several centuries how to make particular wines that would gracefully age for a hundred years, most wines remained local, perishable products destined for use by those who made them and a few of their neighbors. In the last thirty years wine has been transformed from a local commodity to a global one, because we've learned how to preserve wine and then distribute it to distant locations in a way that does not sacrifice its flavors. We've also learned to recognize which conditions create the best fruit and to reproduce those conditions in vineyards around the world. As any winemaker will say, wine is made in the vineyard. In other words, the quality of wine is mainly influenced by the quality of the fruit from which it is made.

So we give our thanks to wine producers the world over who, during these last decades, have elevated the quality of most wine to levels where only a few have been before. We also give thanks to the merchants and importers who make many different wines available in almost every nook and cranny of the globe. We also thank the publishers and wine writers who became increasingly important guides as the choices multiplied. But especially we thank the small producers who cherished tradition and at the same time courageously experimented in their vineyards and wineries so that we could all experience the wonder of wine at its best as nature first delivers it.

Introduction

Who Is This Book For?

Quite simply, this book is for people who buy wine and have more common sense than money. It's for people who know people who buy wine. It's a perfect gift. It's not very expensive. In fact, it's cheap in comparison with other good books and most good bottles of wine. This book is for your friends who go to parties and bring bottles of wine of such poor quality that no one will drink them, including themselves. But really our book is for anyone who enjoys drinking good wine.

We all know a good wine can help create a magical moment while a mediocre wine seems to have the opposite effect. So why do people drink mediocre wines? It's not because they are cheaper than good wines, because often the opposite is true. Mediocre wines can be very expensive. One of the basic tenets of this book is that when purchasing wines, you need to understand that price is never a reliable guide to value.

Because a wine costs more does not mean it will be better or even as good as a much less expensive wine. The fact is, a lot of overhyped, underwhelming wines on the market command big prices simply because the winery has the cheek to demand them. What's more, they get those prices. Consumers assume that if a wine costs more, it must be better. Unfortunately, it just isn't so. So let us say it once again: Quality and price are not synonymous.

No one wants to spend money unnecessarily, especially if you are a cheapskate. Now to be a cheapskate doesn't mean that you possess the mean spirit of a Scrooge. Rather to be a cheapskate is simply to be careful how you spend money. Benjamin Franklin, a founding father of this country, was both a lover of wine and a forerunner of the modern cheapskate. We are sure he would agree that money that does not recieve its worth in exchange is money spent foolishly. In short, it is money wasted.

Ultimately, this book is about *searching for* and *finding value* to make sure we spend our money wisely and well. When there are hundreds and hundreds of outstanding, reasonably priced wines available to the consumer, why should anyone spend good money for mediocre wine or, just as silly, spend too much for good wine? Yet most people do.

While we do not claim that this book will make you more attractive or improve your golf score, it might just improve your love life, might even make you some money, and may even help you live longer, as well as better. Most important, what this book can do is save you money and insure that you will drink better wines from now on.

In the pages that follow, we will show you where and when to shop to get the best possible prices. You don't need a relative in the wine business to get great deals. Did you know that at certain times you can buy premium wines at your local supermarket for less than the wine merchant across town can buy them wholesale? It's true. We will identify wines that are much better than wines costing two to five times as much, we will tell you which wines are worth collecting (most aren't), which wines can quintuple in value in a few years (quite a number do), and where and how to sell them when they've increased so much in value that you don't feel you can afford to drink them. (It's a great feeling!)

We will also give you tips on how to bid wisely at auction, often a great source of bargains. Plus we'll show you how to maximize the enjoyment your wines can provide: at what temperature to serve them, foods to pair with them, and how to properly store them.

A glass of good wine enhances a meal because it both complements food and relaxes the tensions that accumulate during the day, allowing us to better appreciate the time that we spend at the table with our companions. We now know that wine with meals also has health benefits. People who drink wine in moderation with meals live longer with fewer ailments than either those who never drink at all or those who drink heavily. So when we buy good wine wisely and well, the most ardent cheapskate can afford its daily enjoyment and need not reserve the pleasure only for special occasions.

1

Learning About Wines

You don't need to know anything about wine to enjoy a glass of it, anymore than you need to be an expert on the harvesting and preparation of shellfish to like lobster. Many people are quite happy to let others make all the decisions when it comes to selecting the wine they drink, just as many people are happy never to go near a kitchen. However, for most people, a little knowledge adds to the enjoyment and excitement of a wine. (There is a glossary in the back of the book that defines a number of terms with which you may be unfamiliar.) For some, the thrill of reading about wine, of tasting, learning, and educating their minds and palates becomes a lifelong delight if not an outright passion.

Most people simply take a haphazard approach to getting a wine education, but even that approach can have definite benefits. They can set their own pace, gathering bits of information in no prescribed manner and without pressure of any kind. This random approach to learning is enjoyable precisely because it lacks structure. Their goals exist but remain unarticulated and enjoyably vague. They know they're reading about wine to educate themselves, to learn something, but they also know they're reading to escape.

To those who have a nine-to-five life, the world of wine can be almost mythical. If you were to rely solely on articles in glossy wine magazines, you would find a world only filled with photogenic fairytale kingdoms in distant lands. Reading about wine takes you away from office politics, away from committee meetings, away from commuting, and transports you to towns dating from the time of Charlemagne, to terraced vineyards clinging to hillsides, to cellars carved deep into the damp earth, and to châteaux and villas the size of New York apartment buildings peopled by owners who seem to belong to an aristocracy from an earlier time. When you read about wine, you journey over a long road that twists and turns but which need never end, unlike a good novel.

In addition to steeping you in the romance of wine, learning about wine will also help you make more informed decisions about the wines you buy. You will discover that you can buy a wine that costs $8 a bottle that outshines its rivals selling for twice and three times as much. You will discover hundreds of varieties of wine each with its own history. You will learn which foods complement a given wine, so you can heighten the pleasures you derive from both. You will also learn that wine can prolong your life if used in a reasonable manner and can kill if abused.

Sources of Information

The Weekly Food Section in the Local Newspaper

A handy vehicle for learning more about wine is the weekly food section in your local paper. Here you'll find reviews of wines that have been tasted during the past week by staff and members of the wine trade. The wines are described, given scores or ratings, along with suggestions as to what foods will match especially well with each wine. The articles are usually straightforward and concise, and what's more, the wines are available locally. If a particular wine strikes your fancy, you should have little difficulty finding it. If your neighborhood merchant doesn't carry it, a call to the paper will get the name of a retailer who does with no fuss and no muss. Along with the wines reviewed by committee, there are articles by wine writers on a variety of topics: the harvest prospects, a special tasting, a particular varietal or winery, or perhaps a personality in the trade who has left his mark. The articles can be funny or serious, lightweight or profound.

Wine Merchants' Newsletters

The newsletters that wine merchants send out to advertise their wares are free and often actually contain interesting information along with the hype. In addition to page after page of wines, there are usually short articles by staff members that range over a broad range of wine-related topics. They provide an easy way to broaden your wine horizons.

Wine Publications

Articles about wine abound in numerous magazines that deal with contemporary lifestyle issues. They range from lists of wines to serve with your Thanksgiving turkey to long, in-depth articles about a particular wine-producing region. However, wine is only one of many topics covered. If one really wants to find out about current wine releases, their prices, vintage conditions, etc., you are best served by reading the publications devoted to wine; the three most prominent are the *Wine Spectator*, the *Wine Advocate*, and the *Wine Enthusiast*.

The *Wine Spectator*

Definitely the biggest, slickest, and most attractive of the trio is the *Wine Spectator*. The creation of Marvin Shanken, who also publishes *Cigar Aficionado*, the magazine is published every two weeks. It is filled with outstanding graphics and spectacular photographs to complement the articles that cover a wide range of topics besides wine, including fine food, restaurants, hotels, resorts, and anything that might come under the umbrella of the "good life." Understand that the "good life" as featured by the *Wine Spectator* doesn't come cheap. Few of us have the resources to jet to Paris for a weekend of the finest wining, dining, and shopping that the city has to offer—but we can always dream.

Though the magazine indulges heavily in what for most readers can only be fantasies, its main focus is wine. Every issue reviews and rates hundreds of wines from various wine-growing regions around the world. It is almost always the first to come out with an assessment of the newest Bordeaux vintage. The magazine not only concentrates on the wines that demand big bucks, but also does a nice job of finding less expensive wines whose quality outstrips their prices.

When evaluating a large number of wines such as California Cabernet Sauvignon from a particular vintage, it arranges the wines alphabetically and highlights the wines that are top scorers as well as those wines that the authors consider "collectible," a "best value," or a "smart buy."

Most issues have a page or two devoted to the latest wine auction results, and four times a year the magazine publishes a chart following the upward and downward price movements of a number of key vintages of Bordeaux and other wines for the previous quarter. If you are thinking of buying or selling wines at auction or are just curious where the value of your collection has gone in the last three months, this is a handy guide. Wines, whatever else they might be, are also commodities.

The *Wine Spectator* is available by subscription and can also be found in most large wine stores.

The *Wine Spectator*
1-800-752-7799
www.winespectator.com
1 year subscription is $50 in the U.S., first class mail.

The *Wine Advocate*

The *Wine Advocate* is a newsletter that until recently was written by just one person, Robert Parker. It is generally considered by serious wine collectors to be the single most important source of information about wine.

Parker was an attorney who in the early 1980s gave up practicing law to devote himself to his real love: wine. When he began publishing, there were a couple of other newsletters that reviewed wine. However, none approached the topic with the thoroughness and almost zealous ardor for integrity that Parker did. At that time, wine writers not only expected certain perks, but a few were suspected of receiving under-the-table payments for favorable reviews. All of Parker's costs, including the purchase of wine, were met from the proceeds generated by the newsletter. Not only was there no conflict of interest, he set out to ensure that there would not be even a hint of it. How important fairness and objectivity was to him was revealed several years ago when he went into partnership with his brother-in-law in a winery in Oregon. In a message to his subscribers, he told of his involvement and stated that at no time would he review his own wines. Also you will notice that there are no advertisements in the *Wine Advocate,* unlike any of the other major wine magazines.

Having integrity is certainly admirable, but if one does not have an outstanding palate, it's meaningless. Fortunately he does have an exceptional palate as well as a seemingly tireless one. It is not unusual for him to taste several hundred wines in the course of a day.

One of the keys to Parker's success was the introduction of the 100-point scale, which is similar to the scoring system used in schools throughout the United States. It helped to demystify wine because it was clear-cut and unequivocal. A wine that scored 95 was better than a wine that scored 89, even though much of the descriptive verbiage surrounding the two wines might be similar. The score was an unhedged, qualitative judgment. Wines might have superb, excellent, outstanding, or any number of somewhat nonspecific adjectives attached to them, yet if they received a score of 91 versus another wine's 94, the reader knew, that, at least in Mr. Parker's opinion, one wine was simply better than the other.

Other critics and wine writers cried foul. How could he assign a number to something so ethereal, so complex, so full of nuances as fine wine? Parker defended his numerical scoring system by pointing out that the score was only part of his evaluation of each wine, that it served as an additional aid to the consumer. It also reflected his unevasive approach to stating his opinion. Although the 100-point scale was initially disparaged by critics, the wine-buying public loved it. Gradually a number of other critics and publications saw the writing on the wall and adopted the 100-point scoring scale, which is commonplace today.

The *Wine Advocate* does something that other publications do not. It lists the names and phone numbers of the importers of each wine reviewed or the telephone number of the winery, if it is American. This allows the consumer to find the nearest retail store where the wine might be purchased or, in the case of small-production Califor-

nia wines, to get on the winery's mailing list. Nothing is quite so frus-
trating as seeing a glowing description of a wine accompanied by a
score of 97 and a price tag of $27 without having the foggiest idea
where you might purchase it. It is hoped that, in time, the *Wine
Spectator* and the *Wine Enthusiast* will remedy this oversight and also
include this very important information.

The *Wine Advocate* is only available by subscription.

The *Wine Advocate,* Inc.
P.O. Box 311
Monkton, MD 21111
410-329-6477
fax: 410-357-4504
www.wine-advocate.com
Rates are domestic $55 per year for six issues, first class mail.

The *Wine Enthusiast*

The *Wine Enthusiast* is stylistically similar to the *Wine Spectator*
with the same large format, glossy paper, and excellent photographs,
but generally with one-third to one-half the number of pages. Published once a month, most of the magazine is devoted to the evaluation and scoring of hundreds of wines, as well as beers and spirits, with
articles related to wine and wine-growing regions and their attractions. And while it doesn't match either the *Wine Advocate* or the
Wine Spectator's comprehensive coverage of French and European
wines, it is especially strong in the area of American wines.

Because the *Wine Enthusiast* has a smaller reader base than either
the *Wine Advocate* or the *Wine Spectator*, when it rates a wine in the
high 90s, there is every likelihood that the wine will be around for
more than a nanosecond after the magazine comes out, so you might
actually be able to purchase it!

The *Wine Enthusiast* is available primarily by subscription.

The *Wine Enthusiast*
1-800-829-5901
1-800-752-7799

www.wineenthusiast.com
Subscription rate is $32.95 per year for 14 issues

There are numerous other wine magazines and wine publications
that are informative and well written, and though they are fun to read,
they are not as comprehensive in the number of wines they review as
the three listed above.

Books

They're out there, hundreds of them, coffee table books with beautiful photographs of vineyards and wineries, bathed in the golden light
of day's end, serious academic books, guidebooks to wines, by price,
varietal, region, medals, books that tell you where to stay and eat
should you be in the winery's neighborhood. The variety is endless.

Pick a wine topic, and there's probably a book on it. There's even
one for Cheapskates now! If you can't find a book dealing only with
Petit Verdot, there's always the *Oxford Companion to Wine*, edited by
Jancis Robinson, an 1,100-page encyclopedic compendium on wine
and related topics.

Wine Competitions: All That Glitters . . .

First axiom: Wine is a business.

The grease that keeps the machine running is publicity, preferably
good, preferably free. This is the reason that wine competitions,
newsletters, magazines, and newspapers are so important to wineries.

*Second axiom: Wine competitions are not designed to inform the con-
sumer but to sell wines.*

*Third axiom: There are so many wine competitions that if a wine is en-
tered into enough of them, it will receive a medal somewhere, which
the winery then can use to promote the wine.*

Here's a thumbnail sketch of how wine competitions work:
In the interests of impartiality, wines are evaluated in blind tastings,

generally with similar varietals. Chardonnays are judged against other Chardonnays, Cabernet Sauvignons against other Cabernet Sauvignons, and so on. The wines are judged in flights, usually with eight to twelve wines in a flight. The judges make evaluations based on color, clarity, smell, and taste. They swirl and sniff, taste, and spit out each wine, and then make notes about the wines and assign scores. The wine with the highest score gets the gold medal, and those with slightly lower scores get silver medals or bronze.

Bob Thompson, a California wine writer who participates in a large number of judgings both in the United States and abroad, has commented that many wineries design their wines to do well in these competitive tastings. Gold medals and high scores mean two things. A wine will be easier to sell, and the winery can get a higher price for it, if not this year, then next. As a result, we have what Thompson calls the "Award-Winning New International White Wine" and the "Award-Winning New International Red Wine."

"Award-Winning New International White Wine" is fermented in oak, put through a secondary malolactic fermentation, and then aged on the lees or sediment that remains after fermentation. Aging wine on the lees deepens flavors. The oak gives the wine a vanilla quality, and malolactic fermentation gives the wine a buttery, less acidic character. "All the blind tasters have to do is recognize the oak and the malolactic, and they are home free. Chardonnay is the ideal grape, because it doesn't get in the way of the oak and the malolactic very much, but a determined winemaker can overcome Sauvignon Blanc, Viognier, whatever." In other words, Thompson is ironically lamenting that winemakers who aim for this banal award-winning style can easily obscure Chardonnay varietal flavors with heavy-handed oak and malolactic treatment although they need to be more determined to do so with other grape varietals.

To illustrate his point, Thompson has slipped Sauvignon Blancs, Chenin Blancs, and white-wine blends made in this style and put them into Chardonnay tastings. None of the judges realized that they were drinking something other than Chardonnay. Whatever varietal character the wines may possess gets buried under the oak and malolactic flavors. The grape varietal, whether Chardonnay, Sauvignon Blanc, Chenin Blanc, or Viognier, is no longer the lead singer in the band but has been relegated to playing backup. The result is a disheartening sameness among white wines.

In fact, what actually distinguishes one of these wines from another is not so much the grapes but rather the amount and type of oak used, what percentage of a particular wine went through malolactic fermentation, and how long it remained on the lees. New oak barrels cost more than used oak barrels but impart more flavor. French oak barrels cost more than American oak barrels but are preferred by judges. Thus wineries that use a lot of new French oak barrels in which to ferment their wines tend to win more competitions and, of course, have to charge more for their wines to pay for the French barrels. They can do that because they have all those medals to entice customers to buy their award-winning wines.

A similar procedure is used for what Thompson calls the "Award-Winning New International Red Wine." Grapes, skins, and seeds are all tossed in to gain maximum extraction. Then the wine is put through the secondary malolactic fermentation and placed in new oak barrels. The result is that red wines lose their varietal character. Syrah tastes like Merlot, which tastes like Sangiovese, which tastes like a Meritage, which should make choosing a wine a snap, since they all taste, more or less, alike.

Thompson's lament about the style of the "Award-Winning International Wines" is that they don't match up very well with food and so aren't really appropriate for the dinner table. He does allow that these whites pair well with artificially buttered popcorn, and the reds taste okay with the boxes that fast food cheeseburgers come in!

In fairness to the wineries, if they don't sell their wines, they don't stay in business. Many reason that they need to make wines to which the judges and critics will award medals and high scores. So what if they taste like everyone else's wine? That's the price for success. Though the temptation is to lay the blame for the overwhelming sameness of much of the wine on the market at the doorstep of wineries, critics, and judges, ultimately the consumer is the one who buys the wine. An old saying goes, "You can lead a horse to water, but you can't make him drink." Perhaps there should be a coda, "You can't make him anything but Merlot and Chardonnay." In other words, the consumer, for whatever reason, likes the style of "Award-Winning International Wines."

Probably the only influences that wineries react to more than wine competitions when they determine the style of wine that they are going to make, are influential critics and wine publications. And the most influential critic of them all is Robert Parker who publishes the *Wine Advocate*. Over the last fifteen to twenty years, Parker has probably influenced the course of winemaking here and abroad more than any other single individual, in or out of the wine business. Among other things, Parker has argued long and well against stripping a wine of its character by excessive filtering and fining, against artificially boosting the acidity to quote "make the wine more food friendly," and against making technically correct but boring wines. All good points. As a result, many of the wines of today are more flavorful, more intense, and better made than their counterparts of years past, especially in California.

The wineries, however, reading the high scores Parker accords highly extracted wines, figure they ought to get on the bandwagon and make highly extracted wines and grab some high scores. They often go to great lengths to achieve their goal. Some means are time honored and traditional, like severely cropping the vines to limit their production, intensify fruit flavors, or selecting only the best lots. Others are not so traditional. It's been strongly hinted that some wineries are adding grape concentrate to their wines to boost the intensity. So far, no winery has come forward and admited to doing so, but then they don't admit to using oak chips instead of barrels either.

Yet dangers lurk for wineries that insist on making copycat wines. If Bubbling Brook Chardonnay tastes like Cracked Rock Chardonnay which tastes like Meadow Spring Sauvignon Blanc, how will the consumer distinguish one from the other? And at what point will consumers grow tired of Sweet Feet Merlot that tastes like Lost Trail Cabernet Sauvignon that tastes like Underhill Syrah and look for wines with their varietal character intact, whose personalities reflect the conditions where they were grown, and whose tastes are framed by a winemaker excercising his craft with passion, skill, and intelligence, rather than following a marketing plan? Probably not very soon.

Approaches to Using Number Scores

Many in the wine press and the retail trade feel that buying wines based on how highly they are rated with an eye to their appreciating in value is not only unsophisticated, it is venal or mendacious. Cartoonists poke fun at people who only want wines rated 95 or higher. These are consumers whose appreciation of the wine is based solely on the score it received. Critics and merchants alike lament the herd mentality when it comes to buying wine. It seems so unsophisticated, so ungentlemanly, and actually crass. What they seem to forget is the simple fact that few consumers have any other viable means of determining which wines to buy, even more so for people who are just beginning to collect wines. These same critics don't think it is wrong to buy a car based on evaluations in *Consumer Reports*, nor do they feel there is something wrong with buying a car because it will hold its resale value, yet when it comes to wine, they get on a high horse and disparage the actions of consumers who buy only the highly rated wines. Well, as valley girls say, "Duh." What do they expect consumers to do? Buy the wines with the low scores?

Number Scores: How Influential?

How influential the numerical scores that the *Wine Advocate* or the *Wine Spectator* give a wine corresponds directly to the number of cases made and how high the score is. When the *Wine Advocate* gives a small-production wine a score in the high 90s, a feeding frenzy is triggered among subscribers. In the early nineties, several small boutique wineries released their first wines to high scores. Cabernet Sauvignons like Screaming Eagle, Colgin, and Araujo, priced between $50 and $100 a bottle, sold out in a matter of hours. People clamored to get on the allocation lists of the wineries. Those who were unable to obtain any from the winery turned to auctions and retailers. The price for a bottle of wine could then jump from $100 to $1,500.

A similar phenomenon occurred when the *Wine Spectator* reviewed Clape's 1996 Cornas and gave it a score of 96. With less than thirteen hundred cases produced and priced at around $30 a bottle for prearrival, Kermit Lynch, the importer and retailer, completely sold out the same day the magazine reached subscribers, even after limiting customers to three bottles each. Readers who waited even a day were out of luck.

When the bigger-production wines receive exceptionally high scores, the feeding frenzy is less pronounced but still roils the waters. In any case, a high score virtually ensures that the wine will sell out. Scores between 90 and 95 have a lesser impact, although still significant, especially if production is not huge or if the price might be considered a bargain. Below 90, scores serve as a reference guide for comparison shopping, with subscribers balancing score, price, and their own familiarity with the wine as they make their decisions to buy or not.

Because the *Wine Enthusiast* has a smaller subscriber base, it does not have the same impact as the other two publications when it gives a wine a rating in the high 90s. In fact, you can often actually purchase the wine instead of just reading about it.

The effect that scores have on sales when those scores are posted with the wines has been illustrated by wine merchants who have set up displays of two like wines, for instance two California Cabernet Sauvignons at similar prices. When they post that one wine received a 92 and the other an 87, the wine receiving the 92 will outsell the other by better than ten to one. However, if the reviewer's comments, but not the scores, are posted, the wines will sell about equally.

Scores, whatever their perceived shortcomings, have some definite strengths. Scores are simple and unequivocal. It's hard to hedge a number. While critics might like two wines and have lots of nice things to say about both, there is no doubt which wine they think is better if they give one wine an 87 and the other a 92.

2

Purchasing Wines for Less

Wine is many things to many people: an alcoholic beverage, a food, a mood elevator, a status enhancer, a symbol of sophistication and the good life, a symbol of wantonness and debauchery, a health benefit, or a health detriment. In the baldest of terms, however, wine is a commodity that is bought and sold, just like wheat, trading cards, and used cars. Wines range in quality from awful to heavenly. You can buy some for pocket change, while a handful cost as much as a new Mercedes Benz. Not surprisingly, the cost and quality for most fall somewhere in between the extremes. Ideally, we want to maximize quality while minimizing cost. Or to put it another way, we want to pay the least while getting the best. In this pursuit, knowledge is our ally, ignorance our enemy. Knowledge will help you save money when purchasing wine and will also assist you in getting top value for each dollar spent. If you're interested in making a little money along the way, knowledge will allow you to do as well.

Top Value Inexpensive Wines: The Short List

The following is a very short list of some quality wines at great prices. These wines are generally widely available and affordable, and all represent great value. As we have stated, price does not always equate with value, just as the more expensive car is not necessarily more reliable. Perhaps nowhere is this disparity more evident than with wines, but you probably know this. That's why you're reading this book. You see no reason to spend $40 for a bottle of wine that is inferior to a $10 bottle. Here's a brief list of outstanding wines for around $10, many less, a couple a little bit more. What's nice is that most of them are relatively easy to find:

Forest Glen Barrel Select Merlot
In blind tastings, this exceptional wine usually blows away other Merlots costing two to four times as much. The wine is full flavored and spicy with good acidity and a long finish. Around $10.

Bogle Petit Syrah
If you're looking for an ideal wine to go with grilled ribs or other barbecue fare, this is it. Nothing effite or timid about this wine. Around $9.

Rosenblum Vintner's Cuvee Zinfandel XIX
Year in and year out, this wine is consistently the best-value Zinfandel on the market, often surpassing even Rosenblum's more expensive Zinfandels. Why the Roman numerals? They represent the number of years the winery has been making the Vintner's Cuvee. Usually it can be found for under $10.

Meridian Santa Barbara County Chardonnay
With balanced, lush tropical fruit flavors and nice oak flavors, this wine is one of the best Chardonnays under $10, outshining most Chardonnays costing twice as much. And they make three hundred thousand cases, so it's easy to find.

Black Opal Southeastern Australia Chardonnay
This wine is even better than the Meridian Chardonnay. Very few Chardonnays under $25 can stand toe to toe with this wine, which can often be found for under $10 a bottle.

Talus California Pinot Noir
At $15 to $20, this would be a good value. At under $10, it's well, almost too good to be true. Ah, but it is true. How long it will remain at this bargain-basement price is anyone's guess. Talus is owned by Gallo who, for the last ten years, has been trying to shake its jug wine image,

so hopefully they'll hold the price and maintain the quality for a few years more.

David Bruce California Central Coast Pinot Noir
This bottle retails for $17, and you can easily spend $50 for other Pinot Noirs and still not get a wine so good. Rich and earthy with well-defined flavors, they make fourteen thousand cases of this wine each year, so even though the *Wine Spectator* gives it scores in the 90s, you still have a chance to get some.

Fetzer "Valley Oaks" Cabernet Sauvignon
Year after year, this wine is well balanced, that is not too many tannins, not too much alcohol, not too much acidity, but everything in proportion, along with good clean Cabernet Sauvignon flavors. When mediocre, tannic, hot-tasting Cabernet Sauvignons can fetch $30 to $50 a bottle, this wine is an island of sanity in an irrational sea of overpriced wines. On sale at $7.

McDowell Valley Vineyards Syrah
At $10 a bottle, this is one of California's best red-wine values. At $16 a bottle, the McDowell Valley Vineyards Reserve Syrah is in a whole other league, almost celestial.

Rosemount Shiraz
Shiraz is what the Aussies call Syrah. The Rosemount is a very good one, no matter what it's called. And they make lots of it, so it's not hard to find. It usually sells for well around $10. Great with grilled meats.

Martinez Bujanda Rioja Valdemar Vina Tinto
Spain has begun to make some very good wines, and this one at $8 is an outstanding value, easily outdistancing much more expensive other Spanish siblings.

Mumm Cuvee Napa Blanc de Noir
This sparkler just has more flavor than many of the more expensive sparkling wines and champagnes. Retail is $17.99, but around the holidays, it can often be found on special at $9.99.

Fetzer Gewürtztraminer

Another low-priced gem from Fetzer, the wine is spicy, fruity, and a little sweet, a great match with spicy foods, spicy as in hot peppers. The price is $6.99, but once again, often it can be found for less.

Shopping Supermarkets for Great Deals

Supermarkets are not only convenient but often can be the source of truly outstanding deals on excellent wines. Let's start with an example: You enjoy Domaine Chandon Blanc de Noir champagne (sparkling wine to be more precise, but who do you know who calls American champagnes "sparkling wines"?). In your local supermarket, normal retail is around $17 a bottle. However, come the holidays, the price goes into a free fall in some supermarkets. The same bottle then sells for $9.99 or $10.99. On top of the deeply discounted price, if you purchase six bottles or more, another 10 percent is often knocked off the price. Sometimes, the supermarket will state that it cannot give you 10 percent off, because it cannot legally sell alcoholic beverages below its cost. At this point, you cannot get the wine any cheaper unless someone gives it to you. Because supermarkets buy such a huge volume of wine from the distributors, the wine has been deeply discounted by the distributor. And then again by the supermarket. In fact, at this point, you are buying this bottle of Domaine Chandon Blanc de Noir for considerably less than your local liquor store or wine merchant can buy it wholesale.

Why did the supermarket decide not to make any money on the bottle of Domaine Chandon that you just purchased? It almost doesn't sound American. Perhaps it was the holiday spirit that made them do it? It would be nice if this were the case but not likely. The price is simply a marketing device to get you into the store during the time of year when you spend the most money.

In marketing jargon, the wine is a "loss leader." And the nice thing about it is that you are not required to purchase anything else to get these incredible savings. However, the store is gambling that since you're there, you'll find other things to buy. Either way, it's up to you. But look at the savings. A case of twelve bottles will cost you what seven bottles cost prior to the sale, almost a two-for-one ratio. During the rest of the year, you will see champagne discounted at various times, but never this much. So if you're interested in saving money, this is the time to act. And since the champagne will keep for several years, you will have some on hand throughout the year for birthday celebrations, graduations, when you're feeling romantic, or when you're simply in the mood for champagne. And at $9 to $10 a bottle versus $17 a bottle, it's a lot easier to get into the mood.

So how do you find out about these "loss leaders" that supermarkets use to lure customers, not only during the holidays, but throughout the year? Either newspaper advertisements or the flyers that seem to fill up your mailboxes once a week will tell you when the prices are available. The best clue to spotting a loss leader is that the supermarket flyer or ad states that further discounts do not apply, as the store can not legally sell the wine below its cost. Considering that the supermarket purchases thousands of cases of wine for these sales, you are purchasing the wine at or near cost, and saving 40 to 50 percent off normal retail. It takes only about thirty seconds to scan three or four supermarket flyers for wine prices. If once a month you discover a terrific bargain price on a wine you know you would like to drink, then two minutes a month doing this simple research is certainly worthwhile. If you drink two bottles of wine a week, whose normal retail is $15 a bottle and you can get the same wines for an average of $10 by simply spending a half hour of time a year reading the flyers in your mailbox, your savings will add up to over $500. At this point, that half hour certainly qualifies as time well spent.

If you can't be bothered reading the flyers every week, then concentrate on the period a few weeks before Thanksgiving up until New Year's Day. This is when the best wines and champagnes come on sale for the biggest savings. This is when the stores are in the fiercest competition to get you to spend money, so they go to great lengths to get you to shop in their particular store. Valentine's Day and Easter also afford good opportunities for wine bargains, but not on the same scale. Incidentally, if you like beer, Memorial Day, Fourth of July, and Labor Day are the times to keep a lookout for great discounts.

And remember, most supermarkets offer additional discounts of either 5 percent or 10 percent for the purchase of six bottles or more. Nor do they all have to be the same wine. It's possible to purchase one

bottle of Dom Perignon Champagne for $109 and five bottles of some
other wine at $2.99 and receive the 10 percent discount on all six. And
each 1.5-liter bottle counts as two bottles toward half case discounts.

Supermarkets, while the most obvious and probably the most convenient source of wine bargains, are but the tip of the iceberg. Here
are some of the other sources that offer the consumer the opportunity
to purchase wines at substantial savings.

Members-Only Price Clubs

Price clubs like Costco afford their members the convenience of
not having to wait for wines to come on sale, because they are always
on sale. If a bottle of Raymond Amberhill Chardonnay is $5.39 in July,
it will be $5.39 in December or March or May or until the cost of the
wine goes up. Because of their huge volume and purchasing power
plus a markup of about 10 percent over cost versus 25 to 50 percent
for supermarkets and liquor stores, the wines from price clubs often
offer real value to the consumer. However, there are no additional 10
to 15 percent discounts for half or full case purchases such as supermarkets and many liquor stores offer, since the wine has already been
fully discounted. This is handy if you want to buy only a single bottle
of wine. However, if you are purchasing a case of wine from a supermarket and are receiving a 15 percent discount, the amount you save
at the price clubs isn't so significant. Also the selection is not as extensive as it is in many supermarkets, nor will you find loss leaders like
the supermarkets offer during the holidays, but the bargains are there
year round and the prices are consistent. Here's an example: let's say
your favorite Cabernet Sauvignon is Meridian. You will find it at $7.99
throughout the year as compared with the $10.99 or $11.99 it normally retails for in supermarkets. And you don't have to bother reading flyers, hoping it will come on sale. You trade having to wait and
watch the supermarket flyers and advertisements for a known, consistent low price.

But if you are willing to do the minimal amount of research, like
skimming the supermarket flyers every week, you will probably find
Meridian Cabernet, Chardonnay, and Merlot coming on sale one or
two times a year for $6.99 a bottle. Figure in the 10 percent half case

discount, and you will be able to purchase the wine for $6.40 a bottle versus $7.99, a savings of more than $1.50 a bottle or $18 a case. If this is your house wine and you consume several cases or more a year, then this is certainly the time to act. Actually, the savings are even greater, since you will be paying sales tax on $6.40 as compared with $7.99.

Other Sources for Discount Wine Prices

Wal-Mart, large drugstore chains, and Trader Joe's all offer substantial savings on wines, without having to pay a membership fee. Again it's a case of volume purchasing power, with the savings passed on to the consumer. In the case of Trader Joe's, the store is often able to purchase the entire stock of a winery that has run into financial difficulty and is in need of ready cash, so it sells its wine to Trader Joe's at literally firesale prices. These savings are passed on to consumers on a one-time basis. How do you find out about these wines? When Trader Joe's has them, they appear in the Trader Joe's *Fearless Flyer* that comes out every couple of months. If a Trader Joe's is near you, sign up, and the store will send you the *Fearless Flyer* free of charge. The flyers are cleverly written and often humorous, offering savings on numerous food and gourmet items as well as wines. Besides the liquidation-sale merchandise, its regular selection of wines often offers real bargains. Here again, there are no additional savings on case purchases, since the wines are already fully discounted.

Large Retailers Around the Country

If you live in one of the states where it is not a crime for a winery or retailer to ship directly to the customer, we suggest that you get on the mailing list of several of the following large retailers. Their prices and selections are generally much better than your neighborhood wine shop or supermarket. If you live out of state, you are not charged sales tax, so the cost of shipping the wine to you is often offset. For instance, if the sales tax in your state is 7 percent, the cost of shipping a case of wine that costs $200 amounts to about the same as what you would have paid in sales tax if you purchased the wine locally.

Generally, licensed businesses can ship wine within a state—for instance from San Francisco to Los Angeles—but it is illegal to ship across many state lines. The rhetoric is clothed in terms of preventing minors from buying alcoholic beverages and other laudable phrases, but the reality is that most state laws that restrict the shipment of wine are a result of special interests, namely the alcohol wholesalers and distributors, protecting their turf. If a retailer or a winery wants to sell wine to individuals in these states, it cannot do so unless it goes through the wholesalers. If your favorite wines are not handled by the distributors in the state where you live, you and the winery are simply out of luck. A winery in Oregon or California cannot ship you wine without committing a misdemeanor, or in some instances a felony, as it is in Florida, Georgia, Indiana, Kentucky, Maryland, North Carolina, North Dakota, and Tennessee.

Although the laws change continually, if you live in the following states you can probably receive wine from out-of-state businesses.

Alaska
California
Colorado
Connecticut
District of Columbia
Hawaii
Idaho
Illinois
Iowa
Louisiana
Minnesota
Missouri
Nebraska
Nevada
New Hampshire
New Mexico
North Dakota
Oregon
Rhode Island

Washington
West Virginia
Wisconsin
Wyoming

If you live in a state that does not allow the shipment of wine from another state and feel annoyed at this restraint of free trade, let your legislators know. By the way, alcohol is the *only* substance subject to these goofy regulations.

But let's suppose you do live in one of the states listed above and would like to have a broader selection of wines to choose from, then here are some shops that have been in business for a number of years, have an excellent reputation, and stand behind the wines they sell.

On the West Coast:

The Wine Club

With stores in San Francisco, Santa Clara, and Santa Ana, the Wine Club probably sells more wine than any other West Coast retailer. Despite its name, it is not a club. There are no membership fees, no meetings. Just the name and very good prices. It does not give case discounts. Twelve bottles of the same wine costs exactly twelve times as much as a single bottle. Its markup is about 11 percent over its cost, and since it does such a large volume, it is able to make some very good buys, with the savings passed along to its customers. The stores are funky, bare-bones operations, yet with very knowledgeable staff, several of whom are working their way to certification as master sommeliers. Wines are stacked in their cases, four and five high, with the top case open, displaying the wines. Prices are usually scribbled in felt pen on any piece of cardboard that happened to be available. The aisles between the stacked cases are barely wide enough to get a shopping cart through. However, the selection is very large and very good, and here you are likely to find wines, which, because they are highly allocated by the wineries and distributors, are hard to find anywhere else. People who shop the Wine Club are not the sort who pop in to purchase a single bottle of wine to have with dinner. Rather they seem to be wine buyers on a mission. Equipped with long lists, they literally fill their shopping carts with assorted bottles of wine.

The Wine Club also has a tasting bar with anywhere from fifteen to thirty different wines open at one time. Tasting is on the honor system. Wine glasses are marked with a line to indicate a two-ounce taste, the price of a taste is marked on the bottle, and pads and pens are available for the individual to record the number of tastes and the cost per taste. Payment is made when the customer leaves the store. No one monitors the number of tastes, but since the system has been in place for a number of years, one has to assume that most if not all the customers are pretty honest. The *Wine Club Newsletter* is like the store. All business and no glitz. Printed on newspaper stock, it is not likely to win any graphic design awards, yet it has its own charm. The thousands and thousands of wines that fill its pages are organized alphabetically by wine type. The newsletter is also filled with sayings, witticisms, and proverbs relating to wine such as, "What contemptible scoundrel stole the cork from my lunch?"—W.C. Fields. "My only regret in life is that I did not drink more champagne."—John Maynard Keynes. "Wine improves with age. I like it more the older I get." —Bernie Gordon, restaurant owner.

Along with the thousands of wines, the Wine Club also offers wine-related travel trips, wine paraphernalia, books, boutique beers, and cigars.

1-800-966-5432
2110 E. McFadden #E, Santa Ana, CA 92706
714-835-6485
953 Harrison Street, San Francisco, CA 94107
415-512-9088
1200 Coleman, Santa Clara, CA 95050,
408-587-0900
www.thewineclub.com

K and L Wine Merchants

Perhaps the Wine Club's closest competitor on the West Coast in terms of sheer volume is K and L Wine Merchants. Since its establishment in 1976, they have changed their name a number of times. These name changes are an interesting reflection of the changing drinking preferences of Americans. Originally K and L Liquors, it metamorphosed into K and L Wine and Spirits and now into K and L Wine Merchants. In the process, their operation has gone from being a corner liquor store, with wines as an afterthought, to an upscale, polished wine emporium. Their stores are bright and well organized. Wines are displayed on crafted wood racks. Customers leisurely stroll through the store, making their selections. Even if the atmosphere is more rarified than the Wine Club, their selection of wines is still comparable, and so are their prices. The one area in which they especially shine is their selection of older and rare wines. They have literally thousands of older vintage California and French wines, as well as vintage sherries, madeiras, and ports.

Their newsletter, the *K and L Wine News*, is printed on buff-colored stock with Burgundy-colored ink. Well organized by wine varietal for California wines, like Cabernet Sauvignon, Pinot Noir, and so on, and by geographic region for the rest, such as Bordeaux, Rhône, and so on, the wines are listed by price, going from the least to the most expensive, an interesting and valuable departure from listing wines alphabetically. It allows the consumer to see what other wines there are in the same price range and to make a decision accordingly. Often prices are unlisted, because K and L is selling them below the point where the winery would like to see its wines priced. Wineries believe they lose cache if the price of their wines is not up there with their competitors or peers in the industry. However, since the wines are listed in order, from least to most expensive, you do not require a degree in mathematics to figure out that if the 1998 Château Michelle Cold Creek Merlot is listed at $23.99 and the 1998 Jade Mountain Merlot is $24.99, then the 1998 Rombauer, which comes between the other two and has "inquire" next to it, will be selling between $24 and $26.

K and L also directly imports both French and Italian wines, bypassing middlemen who are part of the normal distribution process, and therefore can sell the wines at substantial savings to its customers. The owners often travel abroad to taste the wines at the wineries, and thus are able to find wines not available in the United States. These wines are, for the most part, under $15 and can constitute some good bargains. The only problem is that the consumer is dependent on K and L for evaluations, which can tend toward hyperbole with descriptions like "I love Sauvignon Blanc, and don't care who knows it. This wine has the fresh aroma of green melon that follows on the palate with citrus accents." or "Fantastic wine . . . Open, forward, rich, and palate pleasing." Anyway, at $8.99, if it's half the wine they say it is, it's probably worth a tumble.

K and L also has its own house brand called "Kalinda," which offers moderately priced Chardonnay, Sauvignon Blanc, Merlot, Pinot Noir, and Cabernet Sauvignon. All are good values.

766 Harrison Street
San Francisco, CA 94107
1-800-437-7421
www.klwines.com
Also in Redwood City, California

Kermit Lynch, Wine Merchant

In the university town of Berkeley you can find the store of Kermit Lynch, Wine Merchant. Kermit Lynch was a wine merchant when K and L was still a liquor store. If anyone in the wine business can lay claim to marching to the beat of his own drum, it is certainly him. Imagine a wine store in California that does not carry California wines. Kermit Lynch is just such a store. Nor does it stock more than a couple of Bordeaux wines. Instead, Kermit Lynch carries the wines that he likes. Kermit likes wines from the south of France, from Burgundy, and from wine regions in France that until he began importing wines from them, few people had heard of, regions like the Languedoc, Alsace, Madiran, and Catalan. He spends half the year in France searching for wines, talking with the winemakers, trying to get them to see things from his perspective. For instance, he does not believe in fining or filtering wines, feeling the process makes them shadows of their former selves. For years winemakers told him that Americans will not drink their wines if they had sediment in them, if they were not crystal bright. So he would convince them to bottle one barrel, just for him, unfined, unfiltered. Grudgingly they would do so. They thought, so what if he is crazy. It's his money.

Well he did find a market for these unique wines that he was importing. Restaurants like Chez Panisse found them perfect accompaniments to their innovative cuisine. And Kermit Lynch had an ace up his sleeve. He is a very gifted writer. His newsletter introduced his readers to the characters and places from where the wines came. You buy not only a wine, but a glimpse into the soul of its maker, feel the hot stones in the vineyards of the southern Rhone under your feet. You have a sense of the land and the wine as inseparable. You are not just drinking wine. You are drinking passion, history, tradition, and commitment.

You will find his newsletter charming, seductive, and informative, devoid of cliches and wine babble. Here's an example from Kermit Lynch talking about the 1995 Madiran from Château du Perron.

> All right now, let's go back, let's go way back. Let's go back to Madiran before the creative technicians got hold of it and "civilized" it. Let's go back to the Madiran that often traveled to Bordeaux to beef up their blends. Civilizing Madiran? That is like taking the minor chords out of Beethoven's late string quartets. Hey, Ludwig, lighten up. Yeah, let's make all wines smooth and supple and easy. But what about those times when you are in the mood for darkness, for something to chew on, to gnaw on? Our Madiran is a black wine with a dense, deep cassis aroma, packed with wild fruit, a no-holds-barred Madiran. It is 60 percent Tannat and 40 percent Cabernet. It is tannic. It is a palate stainer. You might need a knife and fork to get at this one. Buy enough to cellar some, because it has a lot of potential.

As well as being a major force in introducing the wines of the south of France to the dinner tables of America, he was also one of the very first importers to insist that his wines be shipped to the United States in refrigerated containers to prevent any chance of them getting too hot or "cooked" in transit. Virtually unheard of fifteen to twenty years ago, it is now standard practice. So don't be shy about asking whomever you are purchasing wine from whether the wine traveled from Europe or Australia in a refrigerated container. It's important to know!

Looking for wines that you will find nowhere else, wines that reflect one man's passionate pursuit for the unique, the original, the uncompromised? You'll find them at Kermit Lynch, many very reasonably priced, many well worth the money. One small note of caution: occasionally Kermit's mesmerizing prose outstrips the wine he is extolling.

1605 San Pablo Avenue
Berkeley, CA 94702-1317
510-524-1524

Premier Cru

Another wine retailer who does an extensive mail-order business is Premier Cru. Its newsletter runs over thirty pages and lists thousands of wines from every corner of the world. Reviews of individual wines are usually straight from Robert Parker's the *Wine Advocate,* the *Wine Spectator,* as well as wine critics like Clive Coates or Robert Tanzer, and wine importer Terry Thiese, whose comments bring wine writing to an entirely different level.

Thiese is a writer of unbridled enthusiasm and his style is rambunctious, often funny, and occasionally ballistic. For instance, writing about the 1996 Westhofener Auelerde Auslese from Gunter Wittman he notes, "One of the best wines of the vintage, a BA-type with huge acidity and a raisin-y concentration; little botrytis; just an otherworldly drama of fruit and mineral on the nose; massive density of berry, mineral and a splendidly regal finish; a firm profound Riesling masterpiece, serious and commanding. The wine should be *narrated* by Alistair Cooke."

Or referring to the 1996 Durkheimer Nonnengarten Rieslander Auslese, "Enormously powerful and substantive nose; signature Reislaner, part Muscat, part Provencal white, part Vin de Paille from Savignin; this car wants to go 100 mph; fantastic spice, power, and drive; two hundred adjectives won't do this guy justice; just bloody superb!"

But just wait until he really likes a wine such as the 1996 Forster

Schnepfenplug Huxelrebe BA, "Fresh and shimmery, honey, butter-dipped chestnuts; the palate is simply *delightful,* buoyant, with frisky acidity, and suck-me-down fruit. I know a secret about you. You couldn't resist it either, so you better not even taste it unless you have room for Huxel in your world."

While great German wines like Theise carries on about are not cheap, they are still a bargain. In a sane world, these wines should be selling for more than what they now cost. But we do not live in a sane world. Not when yet-to-be released first growth Bordeauxs are selling for over $400 a bottle, not when a six-pack of Screaming Eagle Cabernet brings over $5,000 at auction, and not when people refuse to try some of the greatest wines in the world, because they are not bone dry. So be it, but ultimately the pendulum will swing, and German wines will come back in favor, and prices will skyrocket, and you will remember how you could buy a great German Riesling for under $30, and a tear will come to your eye, maybe. Fortunately Premier Cru carries a large selection of German wines. Do yourself a favor, try one, and see how great they can be.

Premier Cru has an especially extensive selection of Burgundies. In fact, ten pages of their newsletter are devoted to Burgundies, a good selection of wines from Alsace, most notably the wines of Zind Humbrecht, as well as a nice list of Champagne houses. If you're looking for older vintage Bordeaux, California wines, and Burgundies, Premier Cru has an impressive collection, with some of the best prices, generally 10 percent to 15 percent less than the competition.

One other nice feature is the section titled Great Values that you'll find on the last page of the newsletter. Here you might find the Altamura Chardonnay from Napa for $3, a Chardonnay from France for under $6, a terrific Côtes du Rhône and a California Cabernet Sauvignon for $5.50, plus numerous other values. These are wines that customers buy four and five cases of at a time, great wines for parties or everyday drinking.

5890 Christies Avenue
Emeryville, CA 94698
510-655-6691
www.premiercru.net

Dee Vine Wines

Located on a pier on the Embarcadero in San Francisco, Dee Vine Wines carries one of the country's largest selection of fine German wines as well as a smattering of French Burgundies and California wines. Their newsletter is a work of art in itself, and the wines they carry are wonderful and fairly priced.

Pier 19, The Embarcadero
San Francisco, CA 94111
415-398-3838
www.dvw.com

Bel-Air: Twenty Twenty International Wine Merchants

With the largest selection of old and rare wines on the West Coast, if not in the entire United States, Bel-Air: Twenty Twenty International Wine Merchants in West Los Angeles is one wine merchant whose mailing list every serious and would-be serious wine collector should be on. Aside from the fact that they have California wines that are so highly allocated that almost no other wine merchant has them nor can most people afford them, every year a couple of months before Christmas they send out their glitzy catalog, which they call *Vintages*. It is a book filled with thousands of sugar-plum-fairy wines, wines to dream about as you doze in front of a crackling fire, and if you have very deep pockets, to purchase.

Have you always wondered what the fuss over the 1986 Domaine de la Romanee-Conti was all about? $2,250 plus shipping and insurance will give you the answer. These folks are the Tiffany's of wine merchants, so don't expect any bargains. In fact you'll find the prices to be 10 percent to 20 percent less at Premier Cru, K and L, and the Wine Club, but no other store can match the amazing breadth of the Bel-Air selection. So if you happen to have a rich brother-in-law who's always at a loss as to what to give you for Christmas, you might put his name on their mailing list. Or perhaps your boss has been dying to try the 1994 Bryant Family Cabernet Sauvignon. Bel-Air just might have it. In addition the catalog will serve as a handy reference in case you happen to have any of these wines in your cellar. If you want to sell some of them, Bel-Air also purchases wines from private cellars if they have been properly stored and are in impeccable condition.

2020 Cotner Avenue
West Los Angeles, CA 90025
310-447-2020
www.2020cotneravenue.com

Cost Plus

With stores throughout California, Texas, New Mexico, and Missouri, they offer a diversified selection of wines from around the world at very competitive prices. No further discounts for case purchases. If you live in one of the above states, chances are there is a store near you. Call the 800 number, enter your zip code, and they'll tell you the location of the store nearest you.

501 Clay Street
Oakland, CA 94607
510-834-4440
www.costplus.com

D & M Wine and Liquor

If you love Champagne, both domestic and imported, this is a store worth contacting as bubblies are their strong suit. Prices are as low as you are likely to find them anywhere, except when supermarkets sell them at cost during the holidays.

2200 Fillmore Street
San Francisco, CA 94115
415-346-1325
www.dandm.com

On the East Coast:

Zachy's

On the East Coast, Zachy's in Scarsdale, New York, is the big kid on the block, with an absolutely amazing selection of the top wines in the world, both current releases and older vintages. As their ad claims, more than a thousand people a day come into their store to purchase wine. Macy's should be so lucky. Many of the wines they feature can be found at other wine merchants for less, but then few other wine merchants can match or even come close to Zachy's selection of fine wines.

16 East Parkway
Scarsdale, NY 10583
1-800-723-0241
www.zachys.com

MacArthur Liquors

Andy Bassin's MacArthur Liquors in Washington, D.C., is about the only place you can purchase California Cabernet Sauvignon futures in the country. Also this is where Robert Parker purchases wine. In fact, his assistant-associate, Pierre Antoin Rovini, worked here for a number of years before joining the *Wine Advocate* a few years ago. Having bought wine from them in the past, we can attest to the fact that they are nice people to do business with. And somehow it's reassuring that they haven't found it necessary to change their name to something like "MacArthur Wine Emporium."

4877 MacArthur Blvd., NW
Washington, DC 20007
202-338-1433
www.bassins.com

In the Midwest:

Sam's Wine and Spirits

The largest wine and spirts store in the United States, with all the bells and whistles, including futures' programs, tastings, walk-in cigar humidor, specialty beers, and extensive selection of ports.

1720 N. Marcey St.
Chicago, IL 60614
1-800-777-9137
www.samswine.com

Brown Derby International Wine Center

The Brown Derby has a nice sales staff, a very large selection of wines from around the world, including a number of California boutique wineries, and a Bordeaux futures program. They also sell cigars and Riedel stemware.

2023 South Glenstone
Springfield, MO 65804
417-883-4066
www.brownderby.com

Other Wine Merchants Worth Checking Out:

The Wine Connection
71 Westchester Avenue,
Pound Ridge, NY 10576
914-764-9463
www.wineconn.com

Beltramo's Fine Wines and Spirits
1540 El Camino Real
Menlo Park, CA 94025
650-325-2806
www.beltramos.com

Wide World of Wines
2201 Wisconsin Avenue, NW
Washington, DC 20007
202-333-7500
www.wideworldofwines.net

Duke of Bourbon
20908 Roscoe Boulevard
Canoga Park, CA 91304
818-341-1234
www.dukeofbourbon.com

Wine Discount Center
1826 North Elston Avenue
Chicago, IL 60521
773-489-3454
www.winediscountcenter.com

Acker Merral and Condit
160 West 72nd St.
New York, NY 10023
212-787-1700
www.ackerwines.com

Morrell and Company
1 Rockefeller Plaza
New York, NY 10020
212-688-9370
www.morrellwines.com

Sherry-Lehmann
679 Madison Avenue
New York, NY 10021
212-838-7500
www.sherry-lehmann.com

eVineyard.com

Wine.com, probably the largest wine store on the Internet but nevertheless a victim of its own excess and success, was acquired by eVineyard.com, based in Portland, Oregon. As also happened to many other California dot-com companies, irrationally exuberant investors ultimately required returns that the business couldn't deliver. No doubt, eVineyard will operate more conservatively and it is hoped that it will provide a service that is attractive to growing numbers of consumers who appreciate the convenience of Internet shopping. The store offers more than five thousand American and imported wines, serving wine buyers in twenty-seven states and Japan.

Many other retail wine sites occupy the Internet, some of which are exclusively e-tailers, but many of which have primarily a brick-and-mortar presence. Nearly every business that we mention in this book has a website, and if you live in a state that allows you to receive wine, the store will probably be able to send it to you.

Internet websites are invaluable sources of information about a huge range of topics. Since nearly every winery has a website, you can find out more about any particular wine that you have enjoyed, including where you might purchase it in your area if the winery can't ship it to you. If you are a home winemaker, you can find sites that will help you resolve problems with the barrel you are nurturing in your basement. Also, a large number of discussion groups and chat rooms provide forums for wine talk, if you're interested in exchanging information.

Wine-of-the-Month Clubs

Wine clubs serve several purposes, one of which is to allow you to try wines that may not be available in your area. They also facilitate the decision-making process by selecting the wines for you. You get an organized presentation of the wines from whatever area the club specializes in, such as California, Oregon, or Italy. In general, the way they work is to send you monthly shipments of two different bottles of wine from a particular winery. For instance, one month members might receive a Sangiovese and a Pinot Grigio from Flora Springs, the next month a Barbera and Zinfandel from Bonny Doon. Or the wine club could have some other guiding principle. If they are sending you wines from different wine-producing countries, they may send you two wines from Spain one month and two wines from California the next.

Usually a newsletter accompanies the shipment. The newsletter can be either banal and cutesy or worthwhile and interesting, depending on the particular club. It can be as brief as tasting notes on the wines or an in-depth interview with the winemaker.

If you especially like a wine the club has sent you, you generally can reorder it from the club by the half or full case for a fairly substantial discount from normal retail. This really is an almost ideal way for you to purchase wine. Not only have you sampled the wine in the best of all possible environments, at home and with food, but if you really like the wine, you can buy more of it at a great price. You can also quit at any time with a simple phone call to the club's 800 number. Here's an incomplete list but a good one. The following clubs range from small to moderately large and are exercising care in their selection of wines. Call for a sample brochure and newsletter. Not only will it give you an idea of what wines they are sending, but also a sense of who they are and what their approach to wine is. Or visit them at their web sites.

Celebrations Wine Club

This club specializes in both California and Italian wines. The California wines come from small wineries in regions throughout the state, including Napa and Sonoma as well as less well-known regions like Mendocino, the Sierra Foothills, Monterey, and Santa Barbara. Despite new technology, premium winemaking is still a hands-on activity much like it has always been, and smaller wineries are much more likely to use labor-intensive methods to produce a better bottle of wine than bigger wineries are. They are also much more likely to experiment across the board with different wines, different winemaking techniques, and different farming practices. They can't compete with the big Chardonnay and Cabernet producers, so they create their own niches. The big guys never argue with success, but the small ones must. The small wineries are the risk takers and innovators who push the whole industry forward.

Celebrations Wine Club itself is still small, so owner Anna Maria Knapp, one of the authors of this book, can exercise extreme quality control over the wines she chooses to send to members. She can walk into a winery, taste, and buy existing wines for members instead of having to contract for a large amount of wine made at some future date. She publishes in-depth interviews with the winemakers in the newsletters that accompany the wines, covering a wide range of viticultural and winemaking topics. She comments on the two wines that you receive and presents menus and recipes to pair with them.

The price is $29.50 per month for the Artisan Series and $59.50 for the Winemaker Series, the wineries' reserve wines. Prices include California sales tax, but shipping is extra.

Celebrations Wine Club follows the same format with its Italian wines, *The Great Wines of Italy,* presenting members with wines from each of Italy's twenty regions. Many people are familiar with Tuscany's Sangiovese or Piedmont's Nebbiolo, but each of Italy's regions makes notable wines. The club concentrates on handcrafted wines from small wineries, some of which are making wines from grape varieties that the ancient peoples of the Italian peninsula enjoyed before the Roman empire established itself. Considering that Italy grows over two thousand grape varietals, this is an opportunity to try something in addition to Sangiovese or Nebbiolo. The newsletter for the Italian wines is not so elaborate as the one for the California wines, but is still informative and well written.

The Italian Artisan Series is $32 per month, the Winemaker Series is $62, and the Collector Series is $112. Each package contains two bottles of wine and the newsletter. Prices include sales tax. Shipping is extra. Members can choose to receive a red and a white wine, two different reds, or two different whites. They can choose to receive either California or Italian wines or combinations of both.

And since we know Celebrations Wine Club intimately, we unabashedly take this opportunity to state unequivocally that this wine club is the best, with the best wines and the best newsletters for the best prices.

1-800-700-6227
www.celebrationswineclub.com

Ambrosia

Originally specializing in Napa wines, the company has now branched out to Sonoma. It is basically a catalog company with a stock of wines, including older wines. You can call them, get on their mailing list to receive their catalog, and order from it at any time just as you might in a store. They also have various programs, one of which features wines from around the world that you can sign up to receive at various intervals and prices, ranging from $25 a month to $92 plus shipping. The package includes two bottles of wine and basic information on those wines.

1-800-435-2225
www.ambrosiawine.com

Gold Medal Wine Club

This club sends out wines that have received medals at various wine judgings held yearly. On paper it seems like a surefire, objective way to select quality wines. One problem is that many of the best wineries don't enter these contests, so their wines are not considered. Also since there are dozens of these judgings every year, the odds are pretty good that almost any wine that is entered can probably pick up a medal somewhere. This is not to imply that Gold Medal doesn't send out good wines, only that one shouldn't assume that wines that receive medals are automatically the best. Remember what we said about wine-tasting competitions earlier in the book.

Their prices are $26.75 plus shipping for a two-bottle pack accompanied by a newsletter. They also have a premium series of wines that they send out every other month. The prices for these range from $40 to $70 per package, plus shipping.

1-800-266-8888
www.goldmedalwine.com

The California Wine Club

One of the first and also one of the biggest of the smaller clubs, it also sends out wines from smaller wineries, often good wines that you probably won't find in your supermarket. We make the distinction between smaller wine clubs and larger ones because there are several that are so large that they are actually public companies. In our experience, you can learn little from them that you couldn't learn from your local market by buying different wines in the price range.

California Wine Club also has two tiers. The price for the first one is $31.50 plus shipping and includes two bottles of wine and their newsletter. Their Signature Series ranges in price from $50 to $80 plus shipping and goes out monthly.

1-800-777-4443
www.cawineclub.com

Oregon Wine Club

This club ships mainly Pinot Noir but will also include a few other wines both red and white, all from Oregon. It has two tiers: The Original Club features two bottles of Pinot Noir or other wines every month with tasting notes for $35 to $39 plus shipping. The Premier Club features two single vineyard reserve Pinot Noir wines for $50 to $75 plus shipping.

1-800-wineclb

Oregon Pinot Noir Club

As the name says, it specializes exclusively in Pinot Noir from Oregon. The first tier is $36 plus shipping and the second tier is $65 plus shipping. The newsletter includes information on the wines as well as articles on current wine issues.

1-800-847-4474
pinotguy@rio.com

Passport Wine Club

As you can imagine from the name, this club sends you wines from around the world. The formula is 40 percent from California, 40 percent from France, and 20 percent from all other wine-producing countries, including Italy, Spain, Argentina, Australia, Hungary, and so on. You can choose from three tiers: $35, $60, and $100. Prices include two bottles of wine and basic information on the wines. Shipping is also included in the prices, but tax is extra.

1-800-867-9463
www.topwine.com

Winery Clubs

Wineries also have clubs, which, of course, focus on their wines exclusively. Membership is mostly gathered from visitors who liked the wines in the winery's tasting room. Each winery puts a different spin on the number of wines they ship and when they send them. One winery will send out two bottles every month, another will ship two bottles every three months, while another might ship a mixed half case twice a year.

Membership Has Its Privileges

There is more to the winery clubs than the regular shipment of wines. Often a winery will send limited release wines only to the members of the club. Many offer 20 percent to 25 percent discounts, while others wave tasting room fees for members or hold invitation-only special events like wine dinners and harvest parties. Sometimes they'll send along gifts, an extra bottle of wine, a tee shirt, a corkscrew, or a bottle of special wine vinegar. They want their customers to develop a sense of loyalty to the winery.

Winery clubs range in size from small, under five hundred members, to very large, over thirty thousand. One winery, Navarro Vineyards, has become so popular that they've had to close their membership and establish a waiting list.

Pros and Cons

The advantage of joining a winery club, including the discounts and assorted perks, has to be set against the fact that the wines you will be receiving will only be from one winery, whereas the wine-of-the-month clubs have a much broader range of wines to select from. Also the wine-of-the-month clubs' discounts on reorders are generally better than those given by the winery clubs, but you'll miss out on those nifty parties hosted by the wineries. If you live far away from the winery, it probably doesn't matter anyway.

If you have a favorite winery and want to know if it has a club, the easiest way to find out is to call. Where the winery is located is usually on one of the labels on the bottle or on the cork. A call to information will get you the number. Many have 800 numbers.

Anyone over the age of twenty-one with a credit card can join, but you have to live in a state where it is legal for the winery to ship directly to you.

If you live in Georgia, Florida, Indiana, Kentucky, Maryland, Tennessee, North Dakota, or North Carolina, it is a felony to ship wine to you from out of state. The problem is a legal issue revolving around whether states can regulate interstate shipping, and it is currently working its way through the courts. No winery is willing to send you a bottle of wine if it could possibly result in a felony conviction. If this were to actually happen, there is little chance that Jess Jackson or Robert Mondavi would actually end up in jail, but it does mean the winery would lose its license from the Bureau of Alcohol, Tobacco and Firearms and literally would be out of business.

Buying From Private Parties

Another source of wines besides stores, discount houses, and wine clubs is a *private party*. A private party can be a friend who has a couple of extra cases of wine he wants to sell or a complete stranger who might advertise in a magazine, newspaper, or on the Internet. Buying from friends has a lot of benefits. The price is probably better than you're going to find in a store, you won't be paying sales tax, and you'll have some idea about how the wine has been stored. If you have a

problem with the wine, you know beforehand with whom you're dealing, none of which can be said for dealing with strangers. If the wine is
corked (tainted by an unsound cork), has been improperly stored, has
been subjected to high heat at some time, or flawed in some other
way, then you are faced with the dilemma of trying to get your money
back from someone who might live thousands of miles away. Good
luck. If you personally don't know the person you're dealing with,
don't! Our advice is not to deal with people who don't have licenses,
businesses, and reputations to protect. The risk far outweighs the rewards.

3

Vintages: Chardonnays, Cabernets, Merlots, and Others Worth Spending Money On

Vintages: Do They Matter?

The question of whether vintage is important to your decision when you buy a wine is related to the wine you intend to buy. Whether a wine is from one vintage or another is insignificant for most wines, though even run-of-the-mill or everyday wines are better in great years, but not much. Vintage is a reflection of the weather for a given year and the grape growers response to it: Was it hot, dry, or rainy? Was it an early or late harvest? Did the grapes have a chance to develop fully, or did fear of rain cause a premature harvest? These and a multitude of similar factors determine the characteristics of a vintage.

In California, most of the wine grapes are raised in the central valley of the state, where it is hot, the growing season relatively short, the yield per acre very high, and the wine is usually the same from year to year. The wines are inexpensive, selling for roughly $8 to $15 per 1.5-liter bottle. For the most part, they are nothing to get excited about but are servable everyday wines that can be a reasonable value.

An inexpensive Chardonnay or Merlot will pretty much taste the same from year to year unless the winemaking technique used is changed radically.

While vintage plays little role in the quality of bulk wines, it is very important in the quality of premium wines that are grown over a longer period of time in much more problematic areas, where the weather is erratic from year to year, week to week, even day to day, and so plays a critical role in the quality of a wine. For instance, a late frost can reduce the crop by 25 percent to 50 percent. Such a reduction often results in wines of greater flavor and concentration, and so a better vintage. On the other hand, late rains can cause the grapes to swell with water, thus diluting the flavors or can cause mold and rot, which affects the purity of the flavors.

The vagaries of nature are many and all affect the quality of the grapes. As a result, some years are good, some bad, some in between. And every so often, everything falls into place: The growing season is long and slow, the grapes ripen evenly and fully, and the flavors are rich, deep, and intense. These are the great vintages, when the wines almost make themselves and winemakers say their role is not to mess anything up. These are the vintages when the wines are worth searching out and buying.

California wines, and especially Cabernet Sauvignon, have had an unpredecented string of outstanding vintages, stretching from 1990 through 1997. Yet none quite compare with 1997 for being downright delicious. Rich, bursting with fruit, terrific from day one, these Cabernets, almost across the board, are simply spectacular. Relatively inexpensive ones are terrific, the best are great.

The 2000 Bordeaux are being touted as outstanding with accolades such as "the best since 1990," or "the best in the last fifty years." Despite the hype, there is general agreement that this is one terrific vintage, with a very large number of lesser growths (read less expensive) turning out exceptional wines. *Our recommendation: Look for the highly regarded and rated wines from the lesser growths.* Because they do not have the name recognition of their more expensive counterparts, you will be able to buy wines of outstanding quality for a fraction of what the first and second growths will cost.

Word about a great vintage spreads quickly and wines disappear in a very short time. Small production wines sell out virtually overnight, while wines of larger wineries disappear in a matter of months. Allocating the wines does little to slow down demand. In fact, it may even exacerbate the problem. Caymus Vineyards 1994 Cabernet Sauvignon was sold out everywhere by the spring. The only place where the wine was still available was at the winery, which resorted to selling only one bottle of the 1994 per customer. Still the wine was sold out by mid-summer. They felt that price and demand had gotten out of sync and did not want to face the same problem the following year, so the winery raised its price almost double for the 1995 vintage, from $35 a bottle to $65. The tremendous demand for the 1994 vintage led many other wineries to raise their prices for the 1995s, though perhaps none quite so much as Caymus.

Consumers who managed to buy the 1994 Cabernet Sauvignons at what must seem today like day-after-Christmas sale prices were fortunate, but also astute. They were aware that really great vintages are an anomaly of nature, not likely to be repeated for years. If you want to drink these wines, you must act quickly and decisively, or later pay much higher prices when these wines become available at auction.

Since there is such a realtively small window of opportunity to purchase these wines, you must know about them as soon as possible and act accordingly. You must place orders early with your wine merchant for the wines that you want, even before the wines are released, since the retailers sell on a first-come, first-served basis. Doing this assumes several things: one, you are aware that the unreleased wines are expected to be spectacular, and two, you know the wines that you are interested in purchasing.

The best sources for this type of information are the publications the *Wine Spectator* and the *Wine Advocate*. Both evaluate vintages from a broad spectrum of wine-growing regions throughout the world. The *Wine Spectator* does a yearly analysis of the major wine-growing regions several months after harvest, speaking with key growers and winemakers to determine the potential for the vintage in each region. This is your first key to getting great wines. For instance, if the growers in the southern Rhône area feel that the 1998 vintage is the best since 1989, then this is an area to keep your eye on, even as other reports about the wines begin to filter in as the wines are tasted out of barrel, evaluated, and given scores.

To ensure that you get the wines you want, get on the mailing list of at least several of the fine wine merchants listed earlier in this book, so that as the wines become available, you will be in a position to compare prices as well as actually order the wines. Remember that just because one merchant is sold out, does not mean they all are.

A Great Vintage Is Not a Great Vintage Everywhere

As both vintage reports and vintage charts illustrate, a great vintage in one place does not mean a great vintage in another. Even within a relatively small area like Bordeaux, one region may have an outstanding year, while another is plagued by late season rains. The two major grape varieties in Bordeaux are Cabernet Sauvignon and Merlot. Merlot grapes ripen several weeks sooner than the Cab, so possibly they all will have been harvested before any rains fall, while the Cabernet crop may be severely affected by heavy rains. Those regions of Bordeaux like Pomerol and St. Estèphe, where the principal grape is Merlot, may have an outstanding vintage, whereas areas like the Médoc, where the late rains damage and dilute the Cabernet grapes, may have a mediocre vintage. And the opposite can happen: a great Cabernet vintage and a poor quality Merlot harvest.

Actually there are great vintages almost every year. It's just that they occur randomly in different parts of the world. Some years it is Bordeaux or Rioja in Spain, others in California, Oregon, Australia, or the Piedmont region in Italy. So while 1995 was a very good vintage in Bordeaux and in the Piedmont, it was only an average vintage in the southern Rhône region.

Why the wines from great vintages are so highly sought by collectors is because from these great vintages come the best expression of the grape and *terroir*, the place where the grapes are grown, that you can find. Though the prices for these wines are rarely cheap, rest assured, they will only continue to rise in price as the wine-buying public seeks them out.

As we will discuss later, less expensive wines such as third and fourth growth Bordeaux from a great vintage will often far outshine their much more expensive counterparts from a lesser vintage. When a great vintage comes along is when the quality-to-price ratio is at its best.

If you are only interested in an occasional bottle of wine and all this reading and research seems both daunting and rather a bore, then we suggest that you talk to your local wine merchant. They read all the press and are very current on these matters. Once they've had a chance to determine your preferences, they will probably be happy to set aside a couple of different bottles for you when those wines come into their store.

Understand if either the *Wine Spectator* or the *Wine Advocate* give a score in the high 90s to a small production wine, your chance of getting some will range from small to nonexistent, because you will be literally competing against thousands of other interested buyers. So if you succeed in getting some, terrific. If not, remember other great wines will come along that you will be able to purchase. The pursuit of really fine wines should be fun, not cause for stress or anxiety.

The Wine Grape

The buzzword when talking about wine is *varietal*, the type of grape that goes into a given bottle of wine. There are several thousand different grape varietals in addition to Chardonnay, Cabernet Sauvignon, Merlot, Chenin Blanc, Sauvignon Blanc. Wow! As though it were not difficult enough just trying to figure out which Merlot to buy for dinner! Since the odds are pretty good that you won't run into most of them, we will talk about fifteen or so of the most popular varietals and some of the better as well as more affordable examples available in the marketplace.

Chardonnay

Chardonnay is just about everybody's favorite white wine. In fact, it has almost become synonymous with white wine in the United States. The grape is planted all over the world and with good results. It can retain its personality under diverse conditions, plus it is a relatively ucer. The grape is easy to work with in the vineyard and a wide range of wine-making techniques. It seems to es- by vacationing in oak barrels to pick up those notes of spice, smoke, and vanilla that wine drinkers like so much. A Chardonnay's aromas and flavors can range from apple to tropical fruit, depending on where it is grown. Its personality is such that it can be blended with other varietals and still retain its Chardonnay character. The finest examples take on the personality of the location or *terroir* where it is grown.

Some of the best is grown in the Burgundy region of France, where prices easily reach $500 a bottle, a price that won't have many of us reaching for our wallets. Fortunately, there are lots of less expensive, though certainly not cheap, white Burgundies that range in price from $12 and up for a Chablis or a Macon.

California also makes outstanding Chardonnay, many on a par with some of the best from Burgundy and generally priced significantly lower. In a blind tasting of top white Burgundies and California Chardonnays conducted by the *Wine Spectator*, the top wine, Saintsbury 1995 Carneros Reserve, was a California Chardonnay.

Saintsbury 1995 Carneros Reserve was priced at $30 a bottle. Considering that it bested wines costing more than $200 is simply phenomenal. Beringer 1995 Napa Valley Private Reserve at $29 a bottle did almost as well. Gainey 1996 Santa Ynez Valley Ltd. Selection at $25 is excellent, too.

If you're looking for outstanding Chardonnays at affordable prices, ask your wine merchant to set aside some bottles of the next vintage for you. These are limited production wines and are not likely to remain on the shelves long after release.

The following wines are also excellent California Chardonnays, but with wider availability.

From California:

Cambria "Katherine's Vineyard" Santa Maria Valley at $18.
Calera Central Coast at $16.
Sonoma-Cutrer "Russian River Ranches" Sonoma Coast at $20.
Chalk Hill Estate at $24.
Lockwood Monterey at $16.

Saintsbury Carneros at $18, the little brother of the Reserve but more widely available.

Anapamu Central Coast at $14.

Beaucanon Napa Valley Reserve at $16.

Meridian "Santa Barbara County" at $10 is better than many Chardonnays at three times the price. Often available at discount in the $6.50 to $8 range.

From the Pacific Northwest:

Columbia Crest Columbia Valley Estate Series at $15.

From Australia:

Black Opal Southeastern Australia Oak Matured Chardonnay is one of the great wine values in the world. With a rich texture, forward fruit flavors, and excellent balance it's an exceptional wine. At $10 a bottle it's dazzling.

Some other excellent bargains:

Penfolds South Australia Koonunga Hill at $9.

Orlando Southeastern Australia Jacob's Creek at $9.

From South America:

Santa Julia Mendoza, Argentina Oak Reserve at $7.

Vina Tarapaca Maipo Valley Reserva at $10.

Champagne

Chardonnay is one of the major grapes in Champagne, along with Pinot Noir and to a lesser extent Meunier, both red grapes. Raised in a colder climate, the grapes fail to fully ripen and develop their flavors and are also very high in acid. This is unacceptable for still wine, but perfect for sparkling wine and Champagne. The French Champagne houses operate under a cloak of secrecy, which would do the CIA proud, and refuse to reveal much about their methods of production.

Whether you're drinking Champagne made from one grape or another or a blend is usually not ascertainable, since the juice of all three varieties is white. Any color in the wine is a result of the red grape skins being left with the juice for a short period during fermentation.

Heading the list of Champagnes are the vintage dated releases. Like the Port producers, Champagne houses only release vintage dated Champagne in exceptional years, such as 1989 and 1990. The best known vintage champagnes are Moet and Chandon Dom Perignon, Roederer Cristal, and Veuve Clicquot La Grande Dame, ranging in price from $100 to $150.

Less well-known champagnes but of comparable quality to their most expensive counterparts listed above are:

de Cazanova Brut at $30.
Philipponat Brut Grand Blanc at $50.
Henriot Millesime at $40.
Paul Bara Brut at $40.

Nonvintage champagnes are more affordable, though not necessarily less enjoyable. Our favorite is Veuve Clicquot Gold Label, but here are some others that are very good.

Mumm Cordon Rouge at $25.
Philipponat Brut Royale Reserve at $2.
Henri Abele Brut at $25.
Union Champagne Brut Blanc de Blancs de St. Gall at $28.

Sparkling Wines

If it doesn't come from the Champagne region of France, it is not supposed to be called Champagne, but rather sparkling wine. Still some producers of *sparkling wine* insist on calling their product champagne. One can sympathize. Sparkling wine just doesn't have the ring that champagne does. Ever hear, "Let's toast the bride and groom with a glass of sparkling wine"?

Back to the point, there are a lot of very fine wines that look like champagne, taste like champagne but are called "sparkling wine." One of the great bargains in wine is the French sparkling wine, J. Laurens Brut at $10 a bottle. It simply tastes better than many of the much more expensive French Champagnes and at a fraction of

the cost. The other two areas that produce notable sparklin
California and Spain.

From California:

Roederer Estate Brut Anderson Valley at $17 is made by the French
folks who make Cristal Champagne. This wine is exceptional for its
quality and its price. We think it's better than the same company's top
sparkling wine, L'Ermitage at $33.

S. Anderson Brut Anderson Valley at $24.

Korbel Natural California at $12 is a very good bubbly at a very good
price. You'll see it for $8.99 during holiday sales.

Mumm Napa Blanc de Noir at $15 is made from Pinot Noir and it
shows more character and flavor than is usually found in California
champagne.

Domaine Chandon Blanc de Noir at $15 is somewhat lighter than the
Mumm, some would say more subtle. Still good. You can find it at
$9.99 on sale during the Christmas holidays.

Domaine Chandon Brut at $15.

From Spain:

Spain is best known for it's very reasonably priced "cavas" or
sparkling wines. They tend to have a touch of sweetness, which makes
them ideal for weddings on warm days when a very dry champagne is
inappropriate.

Paul Cheneau at $9.

Freixenet "Cordon Negro" at $8.

Cabernet Sauvignon

You hear the terms "structure," "breed," and "complex flavors"
used when people talk about Cabernet Sauvignon. Let's start with the
flavors. In young Cabs, the usual fruit flavors are cherry, cassis (black
currant), blackberry, and raspberry. As they age, flavors reminiscent of
cedar, tea, tobacco, and leather emerge as the fruit begins to fade. The
wine becomes smoother and less edgy as the tannins, one of the ele-

ments in the wine that allows it to age, fall away. Only a few other red varietals have the ability to age and develop the complexity of a fine Cabernet. Therefore it may seem surprising that probably less than one bottle in a thousand of Cabernet Sauvignon sees its tenth birthday, probably because most of it does not need to wait ten years to be enjoyable. Today's Cabernets are often enjoyable to drink within a short time of their release. In fact, winemakers have been working overtime to make them this way with new techniques in the vineyard and in the winery that result in a softer, more approachable wine upon release, though still with the capability to age gracefully.

In France, Cabernet Sauvignon is responsible for many of the splendid Bordeaux we hear so much about: wines like Château Lafite, Château Mouton Rothschild, and Château Latour, wines of legend, lore, and fantastically high prices—though it was not always so, at least not the high prices. In the early sixties, these wines sold for around $9 a bottle. In the 1980s they sold for $35 to $40 a bottle, not exactly cheap, but still justifiable for a special occasion. Now they sell for several hundred dollars a bottle. If they go any higher, the only special occasion left that might merit buying one would be winning the Publishers' Clearing House Sweepstakes or the lotto. In an economics textbook, you might find the top wines of Bordeaux illustrating the expression, "rampant inflation." Even the lesser growths of Bordeaux have seen an incredible rise in their prices. The result is that many are simply out of the price range of most people.

Fortunately Cabernet Sauvignon is a grape that does exceedingly well in a variety of locations throughout the world, most notably in California. Much to the dismay of the French, comparative tastings of the best of California versus the best of Bordeaux have seen California Cabernet Sauvignons more than hold their own. In a tasting of 1990 First Growth *(Premier Cru)* Bordeaux versus several 1990 California Cabernet Sauvignons held in Belgium, a 1990 Phillip Togni Cabernet Sauvignon from Napa Valley was judged the best wine, even though the judges thought the French wines were all terrific. The importance of this tasting was that wines from an outstanding vintage in both France and California were matched up against each other, something that had not always been the case in other competitions, where California wines from great vintages had been matched against Bordeaux from inferior vintages. This time there were no tricks, no smoke, and no mirrors.

But what happens once you get past the big guns from both California and Bordeaux? Well, California wines shine ever more brightly. Blessed with growing conditions that allow the grapes to ripen fully, something that happens in Bordeaux perhaps once or twice a decade, California Cabernets are ripe, with sweet, luscious fruit. We often wonder to what end one ages these wines more than five to ten years? Do we really want to replace the wonderful fruit flavors with the flavors of tea, tobacco, and leather? Anyway, here is a list of wines that are emminently enjoyable and do not cost as much as an Italian suit.

From California:

Beaulieu Vineyard, Rutherford, Napa Valley at $14 is from a classic winery and is a good value. The 1994 was especially terrific, as was the 1997. Yes, vintages matter in California too, though not quite as much as in Bordeaux. California usually doesn't get a clunker more than twice every ten years. The last one was in 1988, but when it gets a really good one, such as 1994 or 1997, the wines are, in a word, yummy.

Fetzer "Valley Oaks," California often can be found at $7 and is better than many Cabs costing much more. Year in, year out, this wine is a great value and a good Cabernet.

Villa Mt. Eden, California at $10. The Grand Reserve at $17 is outstanding.

Gallo of Sonoma, Sonoma County at $10 and made by Gallo who has the grapes, the expertise, and the money to make outstanding wines at a great price. So what took them so long? This wine represents quality and great value.

Robert Mondavi "Coastal," North Coast at $11.

Markham Napa Valley at $15 is better than some California Cabernets costing $60. Need we say more?

Hess Select, California at $10.

Beringer, Knight's Valley at $22 is more complex, more robust, more everything, and somewhat more expensive but worth it.

Van Asperen, Napa Valley at $17 is not so widely available, but if you should run across a bottle, jump at it.

If you're not happy unless you're spending $60, $70, or more for a bottle of wine, then here are two that are worth the effort it takes to get them.

Phillip Togni Napa Valley Cabernet Sauvignon at $75 comes from the winery that bested Bordeaux's finest. Most of the wine is sold from the winery, so get your name on the mailing list, which is still open, though for how long? The wine may also be available on a futures basis from MacArthur's Liquors in Washington, D.C. This is not a wine for immediate consumption. It needs time in your cellar.

Dunn Howell Mountain Cabernet Sauvignon at $55. Dunn Howell Mountain sold for $45 a bottle ten years ago and was one of the most expensive California Cabernet Sauvignons on the market. Now it retails at $55 a bottle out of the winery, at a time when other wines are asking for $100–$150 a bottle for their wares. It consistently scores in the 95–100 point range. These are big, dense wines that need ten to fifteen years of aging. They also make a Napa Valley bottling that is less expensive and matures at a quicker pace.

To acquire these wines you need to get on the mailing list. Call 707-555-1212 and ask for Dunn Winery in Angwin, California.

From Washington State:

Columbia Crest, Columbia Valley Cabernet Sauvignon at $10 is very good. They make lots of it, and it's easy to find. What more do you want? We know—a case discount!

Woodward Canyon, Old Vines Cabernet Sauvignon, Columbia Valley at $55 is a wine that can rival the world's best Cabernet Sauvignons in good vintages.

From Australia:

If any wine region can lay claim to producing the best Cabernet Sauvingnon at the best prices, it is Australia. The following wines, which range in price from $7 to $12, are often comparable to wines selling for four and five times as much.

Rosemount "Diamond Label," Southeastern Australia at $9 is one great wine at one great price. Tie me kangaroo down!

Black Opal, Southeastern Australia at $11 is the mate of Bl[
terrific Chardonnay.

Barang Southeastern Australia at $9.

Wolf Blass South Australia "Yellow Label" at $12.

Wyndham Estate Southeastern Australia Bin 444 at $9 is an outstanding wine at an exceptional price.

Rosemount Estate Southeastern Australia at $7 is perhaps the best wine in this group and so is its price.

Though the Aussies do better with their Cabernets than their Merlots, here are a couple of Cabernet Sauvignon–Merlot blends to look for:

Black Opal Southeastern Australia at $11.

Rosemount Estate Southeastern Australia at $7.

Merlot

Merlot is hot, too hot. Wineries are scrambling all over themselves to plant more vineyards, but still the cost per ton for the grapes grows faster than wineries can get new vineyards into production to meet demand. California wineries have had to import grapes from South America and France to keep up with demand. Americans are blindly in love with Merlot.

Merlot is one of the two primary grapes in Bordeaux, along with Cabernet Sauvignon. Merlot is generally rounder and more supple and has softer tannins, which means that it is easy to drink sooner than its Bordeaux brother. Often the two are blended together, the Cabernet Sauvignon providing added complexity as well as structure for aging, while the Merlot helps smooth out some of the roughness of the young Cabernet.

The most famous and most expensive Merlot in the world is Château Petrus from the Pomerol district in Bordeaux. How expensive? If you need to ask, you probably can't afford it. It's that expensive. Other Merlots from Pomerol are almost as dear, a result of miniscule supply matched by voracious demand from around the world. Read the *Wine Advocate*, the *Wine Spectator*, or the *Wine*

Enthusiast, which every year evaluate the current Bordeaux vintage, and then part with your money accordingly.

In California, Merlot has been produced as a varietal wine since the 1970s. Some of the most notable old-time producers are Duckhorn, Matanzas Creek, and St. Francis, and the last is the best bargain of the three. At its best, California Merlot is lush, soft, and seductive. Unfortunately, far too many are as flabby as an over-the-hill wrestler, lacking acidity and enough firm tannins to give the wine any structure. Since this is a relatively new varietal for California winemakers, the wines should get better with a little more practice.

Here are some that have good Merlot flavors without the noticeable sag, though none will be around for the long haul, so don't hide them away and forget them. Prices are more than reasonable for the quality.

From California:

Forest Glen Barrel Select Merlot, California at $9 generally outclasses much more expensive Merlots, and with three hundred thousand cases made annually, it's not hard to find.

Clos Pegase Carneros/Napa Valley Merlot at $24 is lush and rich, an outstanding Merlot.

Gallo Merlot, Sonoma County at $10.

Shooting Star Merlot, Clear Lake at $14.

Blackstone Winery Merlot, California at $10.

Voss Vineyards Merlot, Napa Valley at $18 is underpriced, given both its Napa Valley origins and quality. Voss is a new winery, so don't be surprised if the price increases faster than inflation once Merlot lovers discover this wine.

St. Francis Merlot, Reserve, Sonoma County is priced at $32 and is a wine with a track record longer than five years. The 1986s are drinking beautifully now. Current releases are some of California's best and should age gracefully for ten to fifteen years.

From Washington State:

Andrew Hill Merlot, Reserve at $32 is a seductive wine with all the right parts in all the right places, plus the ability to age gracefully.

Woodward Canyon Merlot, Columbia Valley at $30 is a great wine with more than a fair price.

Columbia Crest Merlot, Columbia Valley at $14.

Barnard Griffin Merlot, Columbia Valley at $17 is a dynamite wine at a dynamite price.

One note of caution: vintage plays a critical role for Washington state wines. There are often significant differences in quality, depending on the year, perhaps much more so than California.

Zinfandel

If France can lay claim to producing the best Syrahs, Merlots, and Pinot Noirs, and perhaps even the best Cabernet Sauvignons and Chardonnays, California holds undisputed claim to producing the world's best Zinfandels. And the best Zinfandels in California come from Sonoma County, notably the Dry Creek Valley. First planted by Italian immigrants, it is not uncommon for the vines to be fifty to one hundred years old, resulting in intensely flavored wines. Until fifteen years ago, most Zinfandel ended up either in jug wines or was made into white Zinfandel. Wineries, led by Ridge and Lytton Springs, discovered, however, that if they accorded their old-vine grapes the same respect they accorded Cabernet Sauvignon, they could make world-class wines. Zinfandels can cost as much as $50 to $60 a bottle, though the best rarely cost more than $35 and oftentimes much less.

Zinfandels are rich, spicy wines, filled with cherry, blackberry, and raspberry flavors. They can be big or medium bodied, elegant or decadent. You should remember though, that few Zinfandels improve with bottle age. In fact, after three to four years, they begin to lose their exuberant fruit, so they are best drunk when young. The exceptions are the old-vine Zinfandels from mountain vineyards, which actually benefit with five years or more in the bottle. The best California Zinfandels are an opportunity to enjoy world-class wines, comparable in quality to the best wines from France and Italy, and at a fraction of the cost.

From California:

Ridge still makes some of the best. What's more, it makes more than a few thousand cases, so it's possible to actually purchase their wines, instead of just reading about them, though it is best to get on their mailing list as less and less make it to retailers' shelves.

Ridge Lytton Springs Dry Creek Valley at $30.
Ridge Zinfandel, Geyserville at $30 is year in and year out one of our favorites. The wine is actually a field blend of Zinfandel, Carignan, and Petit Syrah. In years like 1994 and 1997, it's spectacular.
Ridge Zinfandel, Pagani Ranch, Sonoma Valley at $30.
Ridge Zinfandel, Dusi Ranch, Paso Robles at $24.
Limerick Lane Zinfandel, Collins Vineyard, Russian River Valley at $22 is delicious.
Storybrook Mountain Zinfandel, Napa Valley Mayacamus Ridge at $18 is one of those mountain Zinfandels that rewards aging for five years.
Murphy Goode Zinfandel, Sonoma County at $16 is a blend from four vineyards in Dry Creek and Alexander Valley. It is medium-bodied, full of black cherry and raspberry flavors. This elegant wine gets even better with a year in the bottle.
Rosenblum Vintner's Cuvee at $10 has consistent quality, year after year, at a heck of a price.
Saddleback Cellars Zinfandel, Napa Valley at $20 is the one if you like rich, hedonistic wines. Unfortunately, they don't make a lot, so it's best to get on their mailing list.
Cline Zinfandel, Big Break Vineyard, Contra Costa at $24.

The following Zins are excellent but not as complex or as interesting as the very best, but the price is right, and they're easy to find.

Cline Zinfandel, California at $10.
Fetzer Zinfandel, California at $9.

Pinot Noir

Pinot Noir is a grape which does its very best in the Côte d'Or region in Burgundy, particularly in good vintages, which happen two or three times a decade on average. The grape is temperamental, mutates easily, and requires a long, cool growing season. Of all the red wines, it complements the widest range of foods, even pairing up well with Asian and other spicy cuisines. Fruity and drinkable when young, it develops a more complex flavor profile as it ages.

The best approach to buying Burgundies is to read the comprehensive evaluations in the three major wine publications, the *Wine Advocate*, the *Wine Spectator*, and the *Wine Enthusiast*, as the wines are generally costly, anywhere from $35 to $800 a bottle. However, good quality Burgundies can be found from villages like Rully, Mercurey, and Fixin, in the Maconnais region and Givry, Montagny, and Bouzeron from the Côte Chalonnaise, all affordable, especially in comparison to other Burgundies. These are areas that have greatly benefited recently from better techniques in the vineyards and in the cellars.

Few merchants carry a really extensive selection. Zachy's, the Wine Club, and Premier Cru are three stores that do. Tastings, usually held at retailers, are an opportunity to sample a wide variety of Burgundies before buying. We heartily recommend such tastings as they can save one a lot of expense. Maybe you'll decide that $65 isn't too much for a bottle after all. And then again, maybe you will.

Winemakers in California and Oregon have been attempting to duplicate the great Burgundies for the last twenty years or so. Many in the wine industry, especially the French, feel it is a waste of time, since the great Burgundies are a result of their unique growing conditions: the site, the soil, the weather, even the simple fact that they are French, all attributes that cannot be duplicated. Perhaps so. But then they never expected their great Cabernets and Chardonnays to be challenged. Time will determine if the quest is impossible; however, the search has definitely raised the quality of New World Pinot Noirs. By seeking microclimates appropriate to the grape, by matching clonal characteristics to the sites, better and better Pinot Noirs are resulting at prices that are affordable and have a more consistent level of quality than in the past. These are wines that can develop magnificently with three to six years of bottle age. The problem is supply. Production of many of the top wines ranges from a couple hundred to a few thousand cases.

From California:

David Bruce Central Coast at $16 is made by Dr. David Bruce whose mission is to make great Pinot Noir to rival Burgundy. Each year he inches closer to his goal. The Central Coast Pinot Noir is the least expensive of the several bottlings that Bruce makes, but often it is also one of the best. What's more, there are eleven thousand cases, but even this sells out quickly.

David Bruce Chalone at $32 is one of the top three Pinot Noirs from the Golden State. Put this wine away for five years.

Dehlinger Russian River Valley at $30 is lovely, but you need to get on the winery's mailing list if you want the wine.

Echelon Central Coast at $14.

Beringer North Coast, Appellation Collection at $16 is a complete package with balance, flavor, and complexity.

Byron Santa Maria Valley at $18 is one of California's best Pinot Noirs.

Meridian Santa Barbara County at $14 has all the right things at the right price.

Robert Mondavi Central Coast Coastal at $11 is a good value for a simple but charming Pinot Noir character.

Sanford, Santa Barbara County at $20 can age for three to five years and show you the magic time can work with this varietal.

Estancia Monterey Pinnacles at $12 is easy to enjoy and easy to find because the winery makes twelve thousand cases.

MacRostie, Carneros at $20 is Burgundian in style and Californian in price.

From Oregon:

For a while people felt that if America was going to seriously contest Burgundy's greatness, the challenge would be mounted from Oregon. So far the French are still sleeping soundly at night, though for how long we don't know. As with the Pinot Noirs from California, production of many of the wines are numbered in the hundreds of cases, making them difficult to find. Vintage is critical with these wines.

Rex Hill Reserve, Willamette Valley at $40 is almost a steal when compared with the top French prices.

King Estate Reserve at $35 and with almost nineteen hundred cases produced, gives the average consumer a chance to try this wine.
Erath, Willamette Valley at $14 is quite good.
Willamette Valley Vineyards, Willamette at $12.
Chehalem, Willamette Valley 3 Vineyard at $18 has a case production of two thousand.

Syrah

Once again France's Syrahs are the benchmark by which all others are measured. The greatest are grown on steep, terraced vineyards in the Northern Rhône. Here one finds the legendary wines of Hermitage, Côte Rôtie, and Cornas, big brooding wines requiring years in the bottle to achieve their historic greatness. Though expensive, when compared with the great wines of Burgundy and Bordeaux, they are relative bargains.

Vintage is critical; 1998 and 1999 are both considered outstanding vintages, though the 1999 is more supple and should drink well at an earlier age. In the Southern Rhône, Syrah is one of the four major grape varietals in the famous wines of Châteauneuf-du-Pape, along with Grenache, Carignan, and Mourvedre. The 1998 vintage turned out great as both Grenache and Syrah had ideal growing conditions.

Northern Rhône:

The wines from Hermitage and Côte Rôtie can be expensive at $150 to $200, but there are also outstanding wines at much more reasonable prices. Look for the producer Delas' different bottlings of Hermitage. And from Côte Rôtie, look for producers Francois Villard, Jamet, and Burgaud, each with outstanding wines under $50 a bottle.
From Crozes-Hermitage the wines of Alain Graillot, M. Chapoutier, and Delas offer really excellent wines starting at $18.
From Cornas, look for the names A. Clape, Thierry Allemand, and Alain Voge and prices around $45.
Less easily found are the wines from St. Joseph, but even more affordable, ranging from $15 to $25. Names to look for are Domaine Courbis, Domaine du Monteillet, and Andre Perret.

Southern Rhône:

Though Grenache is the major varietal in the wines of Châteauneuf-du-Pape, Syrah plays a big role in many of them. Also, since the 1998 vintage is so promising because of the success that the growers had with both grapes, watch for the 1998s. Vintages like this rarely come along.

Producers to look for are Château de Beaucastel, Domaine du Vieux Telegraphe (here's that producer's name again), Delas' Les Calcerneirs, and Michel Bernard. Prices range from $25 to $55.

To be sure that you are able to get these wines at the best prices we heartily recommend that (1) You get on the mailing list of several of the fine wine merchants, especially Kermit Lynch who is also a direct importer of many of these wines. Don't be surprised to hear Kermit rail against vintage hype in his newletters. He hates it with a passion. Many of the wines may be offered as futures at substantial discounts to their release prices. (2) Read the reviews in the *Wine Spectator*, the *Wine Advocate*, and the *Wine Enthusiast*. Even in great vintages, there is a wide discrepancy in quality from various producers. Since you will not be in a position to taste the wines until they arrive, you need to rely on expert opinion, because the best wines will be sold out before they ever get to dealers' shelves. After you've bought a wine and find you're not crazy about it, you can always alleviate your disappointment somewhat by telling your guests it got a score of 96.

One more important thing to remember: These wines really do get better with five to ten years of aging. Many are capable of aging much longer. Scores are often given with this in mind. The experts do not score how drinkable a wine will be upon release, but how drinkable it will be when it has seen some needed time in the bottle.

Languedoc-Roussillon Region:

This is another area that has seen a vast improvement in the quality of its wines over the last decade because of the increased skills of the growers and winemakers as well as better equipment. The primary grapes are Grenache and Syrah, which, like the wines in the Southern

Rhône, enjoyed in 1998 one of the best vintages of the last hundred years. Wines are generally less expensive than those from the Rhône, to some extent because they have not yet been discovered by many of the wine-buying public, this in part because they have not had extensive overseas distribution. A case of the chicken or the egg, *Oui*? Kermit Lynch has been the major figure in the importation of these wines to the United States, another good reason to get on his mailing list. As we mentioned before, he writes very seductively about the wines he likes, so you might want to get a second opinion.

Once again we repeat our mantra: Read the wine magazines for guidance in finding the best individual wines from the region.

From Australia:

Probably the only wine made outside France that can rival the great Syrahs from the Northern Rhône is Australia's Penfolds Grange Hermitage. Unfortunately it is equally expensive. However, the Aussies do make a number of excellent Shiraz (their spelling for the varietal) at much more affordable prices. Here are some good examples, most of which are not too hard to find, especially if you're on the mailing lists of several large retailers. Some even find their way onto supermarket shelves.

Wolf Blass Presidents Selection Shiraz South Australia at $17.
Black Opal Shiraz Southeastern Australia at $11.
Banrock Station Shiraz Southeastern Australia at $7 is a very good wine at an even better price.
Rosemount Shiraz Southeastern Australia at $9.
Peter Lehmann Shiraz Barossa Valley at $13.

From California:

Thackrey Orion, Old Vines, St. Helena at $50 is perhaps California's best, but certainly its most expensive.
McDowell Valley Vineyards Reserve at $16 is made from old vines. We love this wine. Unfortunately the winery doesn't make a lot, so it's hard to find. If you want some, you'd better get on the winery's mailing list.
McDowell Valley Vineyards Syrah at $10 is the Reserve's little brother

:h easier to find. It's a good value and a great wine with bar-
ods.

Cline Syrah, Carneros at $18 has very intense flavors from eight-year-
old hillside vines planted in the Carneros region.

Sauvignon Blanc

Sauvignon Blanc is the darling of food and wine writers because it
pairs well with so many different foods. Its crisp citrus and melon flavors and bright acidity complement food much better than oaky, buttery Chardonnays, which are cloying in the company of many dishes,
especially those of Asian and Pacific Rim cuisines. Yet over the last
twenty years, as Chardonnay's star has grown ever brighter, Sauvignon
Blanc's has dimmed with the wine-drinking public. Even though it
costs as much to make Sauvignon Blanc as Chardonnay, lack of demand has kept prices at half that commanded by Chardonnay grapes.
The result is that some very fine wines are available at reasonable
prices. Of course if you don't like it, or think you don't like it, then
you're not going to buy it, no matter how inexpensive it is. However, if
you're interested in a wine with a little zip and complex flavors that
goes well with a wide variety of foods, Sauvignon Blanc may be the
ticket.

From California:

The number of acres of Sauvignon Blanc planted in California trails
Chardonnay by an almost eight-to-one margin. Even more surprising
is that it also trails Chenin Blanc by a two-to-one ratio.

Sauvignon Blanc is a difficult varietal for winemakers to work with.
It is hard to find a bad Chardonnay on the market because most winemakers have read and understood the book on how to make compe-
tent Chardonnay. Not so with Sauvignon Blanc. With Sauvignon
Blanc, if the grapes don't reach the necessary degree of ripeness, the
wine can be overly, even disagreeably, vegetal or herbal smelling.
However, when the grapes do reach the necessary ripeness, these
herbal notes are much more restrained and add complexity to the
wine's flavor profile.

Many Califronia winemakers have been experimenting with blending their Sauvignon Blancs, part of it spending time in oak, and part staying in stainless steel to preserve the crisp fruit quality. Here are some of the top ones:

Beringer Napa Valley Collection Sauvignon Blanc at $9.
Murphy-Goode Winery in Sonoma makes three stylistically different Sauvignon Blancs:
 Murphy-Goode Fume Blanc at $12 is fermented in stainless steel tanks, then aged in oak for two months.
 Murphy-Goode Fume Blanc Alexander Reserve at $17 uses riper fruit than those for the regular bottling. The juice is fermented in oak and aged in wood for nine months.
 Murphy-Goode Alexander Valley Fume II The Deuce at $24 is a very rich wine in price and taste.
Mason Napa Valley Sauvignon Blanc at $12.50.
Caymus Napa Valley Sauvignon Blanc at $14.

From France:

At the beginning of the Loire Valley, Sauvignon Blanc is grown in the two communes of Sancerre and Pouilly-Fumé, which face each other from opposite sides of the river. In great years, like 1995, the top wines achieve world-class status and represent the epitomy of the varietal. With prices in the $30 to $35 range, the wines are exceptional bargains by today's standards. When the weather is problematic as it was in 1998, so are the wines. Our suggestion is to tune in to the critics in one of the three major wine reviews for their recommendations. The *Wine Advocate* is especially helpful because it gives the names of the importers, so you can find the wines with considerable ease.

From New Zealand:

Because Chardonnay has been a huge seller in the United States for so long, it has become a model for all other California white wines. California winemakers have attempted to diminish the citrusy characteristics of Sauvignon Blanc so that it resembles Chardonnay, the easiest sale on the shelf for the largest number of consumers.
 Then along came Sauvignon Blanc wines from New Zealand, unheard of in the United States just a few years ago, but beginning to ar-

rive in greater and greater numbers. The best are mouth-watering, crisp, and citrusy, the very characteristics that California winemakers have been trying to obscure. New Zealand Sauvignon Blanc is so good that, amazingly, that country has begun to change the paradigm that Chardonnay has created in the United States. The quality of these wines is as terrific as their prices.

Two names to look for are Villa Maria and Taltarni; both retail at under $10. The Villa Maria is heavier and more chewy than the Taltarni. But both are excellent expressions of the grape and happily taste nothing like California Chardonnay.

Pinot Blanc

Pinot Blanc, a mutation of Pinot Gris, which itself is a mutation of Pinot Noir, is a wine that for years was often confused with Chardonnay, since the two varietals are quite similar in appearance, bouquet, and taste. Widely planted in central Europe and Italy, Pinot Blanc shines brightest in Alsace, in the northeast corner of France, across the border from Germany.

Producers to look for are Andre Ostertag at $14, Jean Baptiste Adam Reserve at $13, and Kuentz Bas at $10.
California makes several outstanding Pinot Blancs, including David Bruce Pinot Blanc at $12 and Lockwood Vineyards at $11.

Riesling

Riesling is the varietal responsible for the great wines of Germany, which until thirty-five years ago enjoyed the same popularity as the great Chardonnays from Burgundy. A shift to dry wines by the wine-buying public, however, has resulted in Riesling's star fading throughout much of the world. This is unfortunate since they are wonderful wines with great depth of flavor and scintillating aromas. Both the *Wine Advocate* and the *Wine Spectator* review hundreds of German Rieslings each year and are the best guides to follow to learn about these wonderful wines. Premier Cru in Emeryville, California, and

Dee Vine Wines in San Francisco carry extensive selections of German Rieslings. The Wine Club is also another good source for these lovely wines.

Some notable producers are J.J.Christoffel, Walter Strub, Gunter Wittman Eugen Muller, and Kruger-Rumpf. Prices range from $10 for some Kabinett-style Rieslings on up. And up—to over $400 for some Trockenbeerenausleses.

While the Rieslings of Germany range from off dry to incredibly sweet, the wines from Alsace in France are vinified dry. Alsatian producers whose dry Rieslings are good values are Lucien Albrecht at $10, Kuentz Bas at $12, and Andre Ostertag at $16.

From California:

California makes a number of Johannisberg Rieslings. While bearing little resemblance to the better German wines, they are nonetheless admirable wines with a wide variety of tropical fruit flavors and good acidity. What's more, they can be found at very reasonable prices.

Ventana Riesling, Monterey at $8.
Concannon, Arroyo Seco at $8.
Paraiso Springs, Santa Lucia Highlands, Monterey at $10 is one of the top expressions of the grape in the United States.

From Oregon:

Amity, Dry Riesling at $9 is a complex wine with intense flavors.

Gewürztraminer

Gewürztraminer with its combination of fruit flavors fresh from the orchard combined with notes of spice and cloves is one of life's joys. It is also the one wine that goes equally well with both turkey and ham, which are holiday mainstays on American tables and problematic for most other wines.

From Alsace:

Look for the wines of Lucien Albrecht at $10 and Jean Baptiste Adam's Reserve Gewürztraminer at $15.

From California:

Navarro, Anderson Valley Gewürztraminer at $14 is produced in a dry, Alsatian style.
Adler Fels, Sonoma at $12 has just a touch of sweetness.
Fetzer, California at $6.50 is spicy with a touch of sweetness. A great warm weather and picnic wine.

Chenin Blanc

Great Chenin Blanc sounds like an oxymoron to anyone who has tasted the rather nondescript jug wines from the Central Valley of California. Yet outstanding, even great Chenin Blanc does exist. These wines come from the center of the Loire Valley from vineyards around the village of Vouvray. They are made in regular and sparkling styles and well as dry (*sec*) and sweet (*demi-sec*). These wines will age gracefully for ten years or more.

From France:

Domaine Champlaou regular bottling Vouvray *sec* at $12.50 and *demi-sec* at $15.
Huet, dry Vouvray at $15.
Domaine Saboterie at $20 for the sparkling Vouvray.

From California and Washington:

There is almost as much Chenin Blanc planted in California as Chardonnay, almost all of it in the hot Central Valley of the state. The production consitutes much of the white bulk wine made in the state. Yet when the grape is planted in cooler regions where its hang time is longer and the yields are considerably less, this results in some excellent wines with ripe melon, tropical fruit, and spice flavors balanced by good acidity. Here are some wines to look for:

Ventana Dry Chenin Blanc, Monterey at $8.
Pine Ridge, California at $8.

From Washington:

Kiona, Yakima Valley, Washington at $7.
Columbia Winery, Yakima Valley, Washington at $6.

Sangiovese

If you've had Chianti, you've had Sangiovese, which is the principal grape in the blend from Tuscany's largest appellation. The area is divided into seven sub-zones, and the most prestigious of the zones is Chianti Classico, designated by the black rooster at the top of bottles from the area. Originally, the Chianti blend included several white grapes, including Malvasia and Trebbiano. While these wines were pleasant, they were by no means memorable. Today, the white grapes are being replaced by larger proportions of Sangiovese, which is likely to be blended with Cabernet, Merlot, or Syrah. The result is a much more complex and concentrated wine.

Another change that has taken place in Chianti is that wineries are enhancing their own particular identities rather than depending on the zones to distinguish them. Many have created proprietary names for their wines or put their particular vineyards on the label.

Chianti, Chianti Classico, Chianti Classico Riserva, and finally Chianti that bears the name of the vineyard where it was grown correspond to increasing price levels that have gotten higher as the wines have soared to new quality levels. But you can still buy a good Chianti for a reasonable price.

Chianti is not the only Tuscan zone where Sangiovese flourishes. Different clones of Sangiovese have developed in different Tuscan appellations over so many centuries that they are distinctly different. Chianti is different from Vino Nobile di Montepulciano although the two wines are blends of similar grapes. Brunello di Montalcino is yet another clone of Sangiovese, distinctly different from Chianti or Vino Nobile. Carmignano is yet another clone, all grown in different localities from which they take their names, Chianti, Montepulciano, Montalcino, and Carmignano.

From Italy:

The best Tuscan values are for Sangiovese wines not identified with a particular appellation but labeled simply Rosso di Toscana I.G.T., such as Antinori's Santa Cristina, Fonterutoli's Badiola, and Avignonesi Rosso. All three wines are made by top Tuscan producers and are priced at just $10.

The following are well-respected Chianti producers who are making affordable wines. Antinori, Ricasoli, Brolio, and Fonterutoli are also making some of the most pricey and sought after.

Castello di Volpaia Borgianni Chianti at $8.50.
Villa Antinori Chianti Classico Riserva at $16.
Ricasoli Formalae Sangiovese at $10.
Brolio Chianti Classico at $14.
Rocca delle Macie Chianti Classico at $12.
Fonterutoli Chianti Classico at $20.

Vino Nobile in Montepulciano and Brunello in the Montalcino appellation make some of Italy's finest wines with corresponding prices between $40 and $90 per bottle, but some are less expensive. The Rosso versions of both wines can be very pleasing at modest prices.

Poliziano Rosso di Montepulciano at $15.
Avignonesi Vino Nobile di Montepulciano at $20.
Val di Suga Rosso di Montalcino at $15.
Tenuta Trerose Rosso di Montepulciano at $16.

Another excellent value in the marketplace for a rich Sangiovese-based wine is from Arnaldo Caprai in Umbria, a region to the southeast of Tuscany, where yet another clone flourishes.

Arnaldo Caprai Montefalco Rosso at $12.

From California:

California continues to plant more and more Italian grape varieties, mostly Sangiovese, and prices generally range between $15 and $40.

Flora Springs in Napa makes a consistently good one for $13.50, and Monte Volpe and Emilio Guglielmo have very good Sangiovese in the same price range. Seghesio bottles wine from the oldest Sangiovese vineyard in California, Chianti Station planted in 1910, a rich, elegant wine for about $25.

These California versions, while exhibiting a range of styles, are dominated by ripe fruit flavors, more so than their Italian counterparts, which tend to be leaner wines that complement a full range of foods.

Perhaps the best values come from Montevina Winery in the Sierra Foothills. Its vineyards are planted to a dozen different Italian grape varieties, including Sangiovese, and the prices range between $8 and $15, which match the Italians for value.

In many cases, California Sangiovese tends to cost more rather than less. Considering that many California winemakers are still experimenting with the grape and are as yet uncertain where to plant, which clones might do best, or how to treat the wine, we would expect them to be more respectful to their Italian competition. When we compare the prices and quality of California Sangiovese with those of their Italian counterparts, the Italians offer more, at least for now.

Southern Italian Wines

Italy's southern regions include the two islands of Sicily and Sardinia, and the regions of Calabria, Basilicata, Apulia, Campania, and Abruzzo at the southern end of the peninsula. Up until about ten years ago, the south was wasting its rich heritage with mass-produced bulk wines. All that has changed as the south has modernized both its vineyards and winemaking techniques. Its wines are an expression of reliable sunshine and volcanic soils rich in minerals. Today southern vineyards are planted with the so-called international varieties, such as Cabernet Sauvignon, Merlot, Syrah, Chardonnay, and Sauvignon Blanc, as well as Tuscan Sangiovese, all of which southerners initially planted to grab attention since no one thought their native grapes could be interesting. Now that they have proved that they can make fine wines, they are concentrating their efforts on native varieties, often blending Cabernet and Sangiovese in blends with native grapes. The wines are wonderful and extremely well priced here in the United States.

Abruzzo is often overlooked in discussions of southern Italy, but the region deserves full attention. Montepulciano and Sangiovese are the main red varietals, and Trebbiano is the main white variety. The wines retail for as little as $6 and are terrific. Producers to look for are Citra, Farnese, Barone Cornacchia, Masciarelli, and Nicodemi.

Leonardo Locascio, whose company is Winebow, has imported many fine southern Italian wines into the United States. Either his name or the company's name is on the back label of every bottle that Winebow brings into the United States and is a garantee of both quality and value.

Look for Freudi di San Gregorio, Villa Matilde, and Montevetrano from Campania, De Majo Norante from Molise, Botromagno and Dr. Taurino in Puglia, Argiolas from the island of Sardinia, Morgante and Regaleali from Sicily, and Librandi from Calabria. Winebow imports wines from almost every region of Italy and all are fine values, but his southern portfolio is especially impressive. Some of the wines will have familiar tastes because they are blended with Cabernet or Merlot. But most will be made from grapes that thrived even before the Roman Empire, grapes so unusual that many Italians don't know them unless they reside in the same region. The lowest priced wines from these producers are treasures, and some of the higher priced wines have been awarded "three glasses," the highest praise from the Gambero Rosso wine guide, for instance the Villa Matilde 1997 Camarato at $45, Dr. Taurino 1994 Patriglione at $40, and the Morgante 1998 Nero d'Avola Riserva at $45, not bad for some of the very best wines of Italy. A Tuscan wine that is awarded "three glasses" could easily be twice to three times as much.

4

How Do You Know You Will Like the Wine if You Haven't Tried It?

Reading about wine is pleasurable. In fact, many get so caught up in the new issue of a wine magazine that they want to pour themselves a glass of wine. When a writer describes a wine with a string of glowing adjectives or better yet, gives it a 95 rating, we feel we ought to order a case. Yet the fact that the reviewers like a wine doesn't necessarily mean that you will. If the wine is $6 or $7, we might be willing to take a flyer and buy a bottle. But what if the wine costs significantly more? How much can or should we trust someone or some committee's palate with our money?

Wine Bars

Wine bars are a good way around this dilemma of buying a wine without having tasted it first. Most large wine merchants now have wine bars, where anywhere from eight to more than one hundred wines are available to taste. Standard pricing for a taste is 10 percent of the retail cost of the bottle. You can taste a $50 bottle of wine for $5. If you're not crazy about the wine, you're only out $5, which is certainly better than being out $50. Besides helping customers to determine whether to buy a wine or not, they offer an opportunity to taste wines you might never have thought of trying or even have an opportunity to taste. Note: Don't expect tasting bars to allow smoking or have multiple TVs tuned to sports events. Be prepared for bright lights, clean air, and serious sniffing, swirling, and tasting.

Wine Tastings

Wine tastings come in all shapes and sizes. They can be big or small, formal or informal, or expensive or not. The big ones are usually staged by trade organizations to showcase the wines of their members. They can be national in scope and showcase the wines of Italy, France, Portugal, and so on, or they can be organized along varietal lines such as the ZAP (Zinfandel Advocates and Producers) tastings that feature the wines of several hundred Zinfandel producers. They can be regional like the tastings held by the Mendocino Wine Alliance for wineries from that county. Or they can use a theme like "Family Wine Makers." Prices generally run from $15 to $35 to attend. In addition to the hundreds of wines available for tasting and the chance to meet the winemakers, often food is included.

All in all they're a good deal, though with the bigger ones the crush of humanity gets to be a bit much. And really, how much can you remember after tasting over a hundred wines? It is judicious but not imperative, to avoid swallowing *everything* that you taste, a guideline that many folks forget, at which point, they have only thing to remember: Be sure to take a taxi home.

Ads or notices announcing these tastings appear in the food section of the local newspapers. Smaller, more intimate tastings open to the public are arranged by wine merchants. These often center around newly released wines, for instance first and second growth Bordeaux. The number of wines is less overwhelming as are the number of people. The only way to find out about these tastings is to be on the merchants' mailing lists.

Wine-tasting clubs are groups of people, sometimes friends, who get together, perhaps once a month, to taste and discuss wines. They can be a lot of fun or deathly serious, depending on the make-up of the group. Cost for the wines is divided among the members. You might try to get a group of friends together for your own wine-tasting event.

Wine Dinners

Wine dinners are a very civilized way to taste a number of wines. The wines are served with a multicourse dinner, in which each course has been designed to complement a particular wine. Wine dinners are usually arranged by a winery or by a large retail wine merchant.

If arranged by the winery, the dinner is usually held in an exotic location such as the winery's cellar or in large tents on the grounds. Food is prepared by a local star chef. Winery dinners tend to focus on several vintages of one of the winery's prestigious varietals, such as Cabernet Sauvignon, Chardonnay, or Merlot. Several luminaries from the winery, including the winemaker, are on hand to discuss the wines and join in the festivities, which can be quite enjoyable, especially after the guests have sampled numerous wines.

The wine dinners hosted by wine merchants can follow an unlimited number of formats. They can focus on wines of a region, a given varietal, different vintages, a comparison of several regions by year and varietal, or a single winery. Usually held in a prestigious restaurant with a menu designed around the wines, the event is a chance to eat great food, paired with equally fabulous wines. Generally the prices for these dinners are a real value. Another plus: Your dining companions are fun, generally well informed about wine, and more than willing to share their opinions, if asked, or even if not asked. Expect to hear a lot of "wine speak" at these dinners. Fortunately the talk soon becomes white noise, unobtrusive, indistinguishable, and innocuous.

Wine-of-the-Month Clubs

Joining a wine-of-the-month club is a good way to learn about wine, especially if you have neither the time nor the inclination to go to tasting bars or large-scale wine events. They work this way. For a fee ranging from $25 to $100, each month members receive two different bottles of wine, generally from the same winery, along with a newsletter with notes about the wines, interviews with the winemaker, as well as menus and recipes to complement the wines. In all, a tidy, tasty, and educational package. Somehow, it is much more interesting to be learning about a wine that you have in your possession and soon will be sharing at dinner with friends or family.

Another advantage that these clubs offer is the chance to try wines that are not likely to be available either in the supermarket or even through the big wine merchants, since many of the clubs focus on small wineries whose hand-crafted production is limited to hundreds of cases, rather than thousands or millions.

See Chapter 2 for more details and a list of wine-of-the-month clubs. If any intrigue you, call and ask for their brochure and a sample newsletter. As with everything in life, some are better than others. The nice feature they all share is that you can cancel your membership at any time with a call to their 800 number.

Wine Classes

Wine classes are for people who like structure, format, and a sense of progress. Information about these classes can often be found in the food section of your local paper. Sometimes they are part of the extension-course curriculum of your local college or university. Field trips to wineries, tastings, and potluck parties all add to the fun of course work.

5

Notable Producers Who Consistently Make Outstanding Wines at Outstanding Prices

When you consider that with over fifty thousand wineries throughout the world making over one million different wines, the wine consumer is faced with the daunting if not downright overwhelming task of trying to determine which wines to buy. Fortunately, the actual task of selecting from such a large array of wines is made easier by the simple fact that most of these wines are not available outside of a hundred-mile radius of where they are produced.

However, even walking into a large supermarket and facing the aisles of wine with literally close to a thousand different wines on the shelves can be intimidating. How is one to know which wines are good, which are mediocre, and which are just a flat-out waste of money? How is anyone, even a wine professional, to know much about so many different wines, from different producers and from different vintages? The fact is they don't. It's simply impossible. Wine writers develop an area of expertise in which they specialize. As far as the other 80 percent to 90 percent of the wines, they know more than the average consumer, but not really that much. Outside of their area of expertise, they, like the rest of us, rely on other people's opinions.

So what can you do to make buying wines simpler, so that when you walk into a store and are faced with a dizzying array of wines, you can consistently make a choice that won't disappoint you but, moreover, that will find you patting yourself on the back for your perspicacity, intelligence, and good taste? There are several ways. One is to find a large wine shop with an intelligent staff who know wine and who will carefully listen to you and attempt to match a wine from their stock to your preferences and budget.

Another way is to read about a given wine in a newspaper or wine publication, call your local store, and see if it has the wine in stock. If the wine was highly touted and received a big numerical score, the odds are that it is probably already sold out. But maybe there are a few bottles left. The store will hold them for you until you can run down to collect your liquid treasure. You open the bottle to drink with dinner, and sometimes it's very good, and sometimes it is just plain disappointing. You wonder: Is this the wine I read about? Is this the wine that got 94 points? You can't believe it. Believe it. It happens. Remember, critics are human, with biases, preferences, and occasional bad days when they are judging wines.

However, there is another way, and it is perhaps the most reliable as well as the easiest. What's the secret? *Identify producers who make very good to outstanding wines across the entire range of their production.* This way, no matter what wine varietal you choose, whether a Cabernet Sauvignon, a Chardonnay, a Sangiovese, Merlot, or Sauvignon Blanc, you'll be likely to get a good bottle of wine without having to go through the angst and uncertainty of buying a dud.

Here is a list of wine producers who not only make consistently excellent wines at reasonable prices, but who have a large enough distribution throughout the United States so that you are likely to be able to find them near where you live. We're defining "reasonable" as a bottle of wine costing $15 or less.

The list is somewhat long, maybe twenty wineries and producers, but all are good, with a consistent level of quality in each of the different wines they make. Although we are not arguing that you should buy only from the producers on this list, we do maintain, that if you don't want to go wrong, you will rarely be disappointed if you stay with the wineries on this list.

American Wine Producers

The premium wine regions in California generally nestle in the hills and valleys along the coast from Mendocino, Sonoma, Napa, and Santa Cruz counties in the north, to Monterey, San Luis Obispo, and Santa Barbara counties along the central coast. Mostly what these regions have in common are the cooling influences of the Pacific Ocean, the fog, and the breezes, which mitigate the heat during the growing season and extend the length of time that grapes can remain on the vine, creating the complex flavors that characterize fine wine. In addition to the coastal wine-growing regions, the vineyards in the foothills of the Sierra mountains benefit from a similar phenomenon. The cold air from the snow-clad mountains slides down at night to cool the vineyards and extends the growing season, resulting in grapes with depth and character.

Fetzer Vineyards

Fetzer Vineyards in Mendocino County is an outstanding producer with wide distribution and an impressive line of fine wines. Their Gewürztraminer is fruity, vibrant, and slightly sweet, a perfect foil to spicy foods such as Mexican, Hunan, or Thai. It is also a wonderful wine for warm summer afternoons or for picnics in the shade of a tree. Normal retail is generally in the $6 to $7 range, but you can find the wine on special for $4.99 a bottle. Often stores will offer an additional 10 percent off for six bottles or more, bringing the per bottle price down to $4.50. Such a deal!

Fetzer's Valley Oaks Cabernet Sauvignon at $8.99 is often better than their more expensive Cab. Go figure. Sundial Chardonnay, Proprietors Zinfandel, and Eagle Peak Merlot at $9 a bottle are extremely good values, even more so when they are discounted to $6.99. At $10.99 the Mendocino Barrel Select Chardonnay is spectacular, easily outclassing many Chardonnays in the $25 to $30 range. It is a wine with a spicy vanilla aroma, excellent balance, rich flavors, and a long finish.

Lockwood Winery

Lockwood Winery located in Monterey County has an extensive as well as impressive line of excellent and reasonably priced wines, all produced from estate vineyards. Steven Pessagno, the winemaker, crafts his wines to be ready to drink when purchased, yet the whites will drink well for several years and the reds for up to ten years. He feels if the wines are harmonious when young, this harmony among the various components of fruit, tannins, and acidity not only will allow the wine to taste wonderful when young, but hold up in the bottle for a long time.

Lockwood Winery makes two Chardonnays, Cabernet Sauvignon, Merlot, Sangiovese, plus several other wines. One of their most interesting wines is their Pinot Blanc, which comes from vineyards at the base of the Santa Lucia Mountains. The wine has tremendous fruit extraction with flavors of peach and pineapple and with toasty oak nuances. It is soft, velvety, and elegant and, most important, pairs with a diverse array of foods such as pasta, chicken, and seafood. As Joe Bob Briggs says, "Check it out."

Beaulieu Vineyards (BV)

While most California wineries were not even in existence twenty-five years ago, Beaulieu Winery can boast of having been around for more than seventy-five years. Founded by Georges de Latour, its Private Reserve Cabernet Sauvignon is still the benchmark by which great California Cabernets are measured. Cabs from 1974, 1976, and 1979 are still wonderful, the epitomy of great California Cabernet Sauvignon. If people who know the wines were given the choice between drinking a first growth Bordeaux from the great 1982 vintage, or a 1976 BV Private Reserve, many would choose the 1976. Now understand that the 1976 BV Private Reserve is not cheap at about $150, but compared with the $500 or more that you would spend for the first growth Bordeaux, you can see that we are talking about a bargain here. Well, almost.

However, we are not interested in spending $100 or more for a wine right now. We're looking for wines that are under $15. In the last four or five years, Beaulieu Vineyards has found the form of its glory days in the sixties and seventies when it was *the* winery in California. Today the winery is not only producing terrific high-end wines like the Private Reserve Cabernet, but also terrific, affordable wines like the Rutherford Cabernet Sauvignon, which can be found for $14 in many outlets like Costco.

The wines are ready to drink now yet are capable of aging for ten to fifteen years. BV also produces balanced, creamy textured Chardonnays, crisp, fruity Sauvignon Blancs, as well as spicy Zinfandels and velvety Pinot Noirs. This is a winery on a roll.

Château Souverain

Another winery with impressive credentials and a wonderful line of wines at decent prices is Château Souverain. It, too, has a pretty impressive track record. Its 1974 Cabernet Sauvignon is still outstanding, one of the best Cabernets from a banner year. Today Souverain is under the Beringer Wine Estates umbrella, but the quality and prices of its wines are still great. With vineyards located in one of the premier grape-growing regions of Sonoma County, their Cabernets and Chardonnays are delicious and affordable, as is the rest of their fine list of wines.

Unfortunately, they recently raised the price for their Cabernet Sauvignon to $17 a bottle from less than $14 about two years ago. In a good vintage it is still an outstanding value.

Meridian Vineyards

The central coast of California has several outstanding wineries producing quality wines across a broad spectrum of varieties. One winery to look for is Meridian Vineyards, established in 1984 in the Paso Robles area seventy-five miles north of Santa Barbara, and now owned by Wolff Blass, an Australian winery. Delicious, affordable Chardonnays and well-balanced, richly flavored Cabernet Sauvignons are the winery's strength and constitute the bulk of their production. Production is well over one hundred thousand cases a year, so finding Meridian's wines should not pose a problem. Normally retailing in the $11 per bottle range, they go on sale in the supermarkets several times a year for $7.99 a bottle, the price the large discount wine retailers like

K and L in San Francisco and the Wine Club in Santa Ana usually sell them for.

The Cabernet Sauvignon retails at $11, and is worth looking for in good years. Meridian also produces a tasty Santa Barbara County Pinot Noir with black cherry, plum, and berry flavors. It is dark and rich with mild tannins, a perfect accompaniment to roast lamb or duck.

Rabbit Ridge

Another favorite winery is Rabbit Ridge, located in the Dry Creek Valley of Sonoma. Owners Daryl Simmons and Eric Russell bottle a plethora of wines, some extremely reasonable for the quality that one finds in the bottle. Forty acres of estate vineyards planted to Cabernet Sauvignon, Cabernet Franc, Zinfandel, Chardonnay, and Sauvignon Blanc forms what they call their "staples." These they augment with purchased grapes, primarily Rhone and Italian varietals. Using eighteen different grape varietals, Rabbit Ridge usually bottles twenty-five different wines in a given year, ranging from a delightful Rhone blend, which they call Allure and sell for around $7, to a variety of Zinfandel bottlings ranging in price from the Rabbit Ridge Sonoma Zinfandel at $14 to the vineyard-designated Zins at around $25. They also make a Sangiovese, a Tuscan blend called Montepiano, and a Barbera.

Well-known and respected by the old-time grape growers in the area, who often bring them small lots of grapes from a few acres of an old-vine varietal, knowing that they will be delighted to make a couple hundred cases of unique and special wine. No corporate rule-book mentality here, nor master-marketing scenario. Only originality, craftsmanship, and the thrill that comes from making exciting wines.

Bonny Doon

Without a doubt, there is no winery more unusual than Bonny Doon or any winemaker more iconoclastic than Randal Graham, one of the first in the group that came to be known as the California Rhone Rangers. Graham might be considered a visionary, a propagandist for the unique and the different, and a ranter against sameness. The wines that he chooses to make are often from grape varietals many people have never heard of, let alone tasted. Varietals like Pinot

Meunier, Roussanne, Grenache, Pinot Blanc, Refosco, and Malvasia Bianca. And from varietals that have dropped from grace like so many fallen angels, such as Riesling and Gewürztraminer, and styles that "serious wine drinkers" dismiss out of hand, like Rose.

In the hands of a lesser personality and a less-gifted winemaker, such an approach might be a surefire recipe for bankruptcy. Yet Bonny Doon continues to grow and attract fans in ever-increasing numbers, primarily because the wines are not only very good but are also reasonably priced. When asked why he has not raised his prices at the same pace as many other California wineries, he replied, "I have shame." We wish this feeling were shared by more winery owners.

Most of the wines are in the $10 to $18 range, though some are less, and some are more. Whatever their price, they are a good value for the money.

Graham wants his wines to reflect the grapes they were made from, where they were grown, and the conditions of weather, soil, and terrain, as well as the people who grew them and the people who made them. So there is no Chardonnay that has gone through malolactic fermentation, has sat on the lees for maximum extraction, and then has been aged in oak, so it can taste like every other Chardonnay on the supermarket shelf. Instead these are unique wines that are true to their type yet as individual as their winemaker.

Just how individual Randal Graham's approach is, might be glimpsed from how he describes his wine, in this case the Pacific Rim Gewürztraminer.

> There is something remarkably decadent, verging upon the politically incorrect about the Gewürztraminer grape. It is as if nature has been wildly prodigal, dispensing far more haunting, seductive aroma than is strictly required to do the job, whatever that job may be—complement a dish of *choucroute* [sauerkraut], entice a young bairn out to the edge of the schoolyard fence, whatever. We have reprised the unorthodox technique of fermentation in brand-spanking (steady, man) new Vosages (keeping it in the neighborhood) pucheons. This little nymphet (sorry) fresh, young, dry, insanely aromatic white wine, is a superb complement to all manner of *charcuterie* [pork].

Wine for Graham is more than pH, brix, and alcohol. It is philosophy, rapture, pain, dedication, fun—and words. Here is another example. This time he discourses on the Bonny Doon Cardinal Zinfandel.

The Boony Doon cellar catechism proposes methods for producing wines, which are powerfully yet delicately perfumed, sensually textured, liquorously fruity, living in perfect harmony with you and your olfactors. This estimable product sees the confluence of those maxims and the full frontal zinfandelia obtained in a few perilously stressed vineyards spread about our empire. The cynic, if he deigns to take a moment and wash the Rutherford dust off his remaining taste buds, may find the rampant pluminess, the almondine perfume, the kirschwasserosity, the lascivious ripeness, and the, lets just come out and say it, the utter paucity of desiccatory noxiousness *pas tres catholique* [not very Catholic] if not downright zinfull. I confess.

Some of Bonny Doon's wines might find their way to a store near you, though most won't. However, the winery does ship. The folks there are genuinely nice and will accommodate any reasonable request such as making up mixed cases or six-packs or whatever. You can call or write to get on their mailing list. Every three months Randal Graham sends out a multipage newsletter—a tract on philosophy, wine, the state of the world, and whatever else he wishes to put on his reader's intellectual plate. Even if you find him hard to appreciate, and you will not be alone, we assure you, you will not feel the same about his wines. They are, quite simply, very good. Here's the phone number and address.

Bonny Doon Vineyard
10 Pine Flat Road
Santa Cruz, CA 95060
831-425-4518

Bogle Winery

Few people equate premium wines with the central valley of California, where high heat and a short growing season produce undistinguished wines. There is an exception that few consumers are aware of. It is Bogle Winery, near the town of Clarksburg in the Sacramento Valley, midway between the coast and the Sierra foothills, where it is surrounded by a system of levees to hold back the Sacramento River. The river cuts through the coastal mountain ranges and empties into San Francisco Bay on its way to the Pacific Ocean, allowing the cooler air from the ocean to penetrate the region. The river itself, its tributaries, backwaters, and sloughs provide further cooling, so that the heat summation of the area resembles Calistoga at the northern end of the Napa Valley rather than the rest of the central valley where it is located.

Bogle Winery produces an array of superb wines and all but the Reserve Cabernet Sauvignon are priced at under $10. In terms of the price-to-quality ratio, there are few California wineries that are comparable; however, its case production is relatively small, so its distribution is limited. Nevertheless, its wines are definitely worth keeping an eye out for. The line of wines includes Merlot, Cabernet Sauvignon, Zinfandel, Chardonnay, Sauvignon Blanc, and Petit Sirah. The Petit Sirah has bright cherry and jammy raspberry flavors with subtle black pepper and spice notes. Normally Petit Sirah requires five to ten years of bottle age to tame its tannins, but the tannins in the Bogle Petite Sirah are soft, even lush, so that the wine is absolutely enjoyable upon release. How long the wine will age is anybody's guess, but the wine is so good, it's hard to imagine why anyone would want to wait.

The Sauvignon Blanc is another delightful wine. When grown in the right soils and climate, Sauvignon Blanc grapes develop a wide spectrum of fruit flavors, ranging from citrus to melon. This wine has intense fruit with mouth-watering aromatics and matches wonderfully with a wide variety of lighter foods.

Hess Winery

Tucked away in the Mayacamus Mountains on the western side of the Napa Valley is the Hess Winery, owned by a Swiss industrialist and art collector. Several very large rooms in the winery are devoted to exhibiting pieces from Mr. Hess's very impressive art collection, which visitors are welcome to view. Not only does Mr. Hess collect fine art, he also makes fine wine. His reserve Cabernet Sauvignon and Chardonnay are outstanding, but also expensive. Fortunately he makes a second tier Cabernet and Chardonnay, which he sells under the Hess Select designation. Retailing in the $10 to $12 range, they are exceptional wines at exceptionally good prices, especially the Hess Select Cabernet Sauvignon. And the good news is that he makes quite a bit of both so they should be relatively easy to find.

Belvedere Winery

On the other side of the Mayacamus Mountain range, in Dry Creek Valley in Sonoma is Belvedere Winery, owned by Bill Hambricht of the investment firm of Hambricht and Quist. Up until a few years ago, Eric Russell, the winemaker at Rabbit Ridge, was also making the wines here and helped establish Belvedere's reputation. With his departure the winery has not missed a beat and continues to produce excellent Zinfandel, Cabernet Sauvignon, Merlot, and two exceptional Chardonnays, all falling in the $15-a-bottle range. The Russian River Valley Chardonnay has a creamy texture, with lots of apple and spice flavors, and good acidity, while the Sonoma Valley Chardonnay is leaner but with more complex flavors.

Estancia Winery

Estancia Winery has extensive vineyard holdings in the Alexander Valley of Sonoma County where it grows Cabernet Sauvignon, Cabernet Franc, Merlot, and Sangiovese. In the Pinnacles region in Monterery County its vineyards grow Chardonnay, Fume Blanc, and Pinot Noir. Priced in the $10 to $15 range, they are, year in and year out, delicious, affordable, and widely available.

The Estancia "Pinnacles" Chardonnay is put through complete malolactic fermentation in a combination of stainless steel tanks and American oak barrels that results in a wine with fresh fruit flavors framed by notes of vanilla and toasted butterscotch.

Its Cabernet Sauvignon has lush berry flavors and supple tannins, providing immediate enjoyment. If you like Pinot Noir, yet find it difficult to pay $30 to $40, look for Estancia's "Pinnacles" Pinot Noir. The grapes come from some of the oldest vineyards in Monterey County.

With a nose of cherry and strawberry, these flavors are carried through in the wine with added notes of toast, vanilla, and smoke. This is a rich, complex wine at an amazing price of around $12. Another notable offering from Estancia is its Meritage Red Alexander Valley, a blend of Bordeaux varietals, including Cabernet Sauvignon, Merlot, and Cabernet Franc. Rich, lush, and wonderful are a few words that come to mind when sipping this wine. It is worth every penny of its $28 price tag. The 1995 was voted one of *Wine Spectator*'s top 100 wines in the world in 1997.

Columbia Crest Winery

Leaving California, we head to the Pacific Northwest and Washington State. Columbia Crest Winery makes both a very good and also an outstanding Chardonnay. The very good Chardonnay, Columbia Crest Columbia Valley Chardonnay, is a partially barrel-fermented gem that retails at $9 but can often be found on sale or at the big discount outlets at $4.99 a bottle. The Columbia Crest Columbia Valley Estate Series Chardonnay costs about $14 and about twenty thousand cases are made each year. The *Wine Spectator* rated the Columbia Estate Chard at 91 and described it as, "Silky smooth, elegant, and nicely layered with nutmeg, nectarine, and apple flavors that linger on the finish." It kind of reminds one of a character in a Raymond Chandler detective novel. Columbia Crest's Columbia Valley Merlot at $16 is an outstanding wine. Since the winery makes over 150,000 cases of this spicy, chocolaty-tasting wine, you should not have any trouble locating some, nor should you have to Indian-wrestle other customers for the last two bottles. The very palatable Columbia Crest Columbia Valley Cabernet Sauvignon is rich in fruit and spice flavors.

French Wine Producers

Georges Duboeuf

There is no wine label in either the New or Old World that can compete with France's Georges Duboeuf in the number of wines of excellent to outstanding quality he produces each year at affordable prices.

For instance, he offers seven different Beaujolais at $9 to $12; three Côtes du Rhône, all at around $7; five Cabernet Sauvignons or Merlots ranging from $6 to $7; four Chardonnays between $6 and $8; a Sauvignon Blanc at $6; and a Viognier at $9. Since it is widely distributed in the United States, you shouldn't have any trouble finding some of Georges Duboeuf's extraordinary wines. One note of caution: These wines are *not* for aging and should be drunk within three years of the vintage date on the bottle. Much of their charm lies in their bright, crisp, fruit flavors, so buy and enjoy them sooner rather than later.

Australian Wine Producers

Rosemount and Lindemans

Like your wines from Down Under? Look to Rosemount for big, broad-shouldered red wines and Lindemans for lush, richly textured whites. Both wineries provide copious amounts of quality, value, and consistency.

The Rosemount South Australia Shiraz is rich and packed with cherry and plum flavors. Drinkable when purchased, it does well with a few years of bottle age. The Rosemount Southeastern Australia Shiraz-Cabernet Sauvignon at $9 a bottle is a good bargain. Production of the Shiraz is seventy-five thousand cases while the Shiraz–Cabernet Sauvignon is over one hundred twenty-five thousand cases, so they should prove relatively easy to find.

The Cabernet Sauvignons from Rosemount may constitute the best bargains in the world for this grape varietal. Ranging in price from $7 to $12 a bottle they are outstanding wines at better than reasonable prices.

Lindemans Padthaway Chardonnay at $13 is a world-class chardonnay with tropical fruit and spice in a stylish package that will evolve over several years. Along with outstanding whites, Lindemans make a pleasant, ready-to-drink Shiraz South Australia Bin 50 that retails in the $8 range and is perfect for barbecued foods.

6

Serving Wine

If you enjoy drinking ice-cold red wine out of your favorite cracked mug while eating a banana split, it is not our intention to cast aspersions on what gives you pleasure. We are not your parents nor are we wine cops. However, since you have paid money, usually hard earned, for the wine you drink, it is not a bad idea to maximize the return on your investment by following some simple guidelines that will add to your enjoyment.

Temperature

Red wines are best served at room temperature. This generally means 60 to 65 degrees Fahrenheit. That means if you like your living room hot enough to raise orchids and other tropical plants, and the red wine you are serving is the same as the room temperature, the wine will be too warm for you to get maximum enjoyment. It will taste dull and heavy and probably flabby.

There are two notable exceptions to serving red wine at between 60 to 65 degrees. The first is hot mulled red wine on a winter evening, which doesn't taste much like wine anyway. The second is slightly chilled red wine on a hot summer day at a barbecue. On such an occasion, the wine must be refreshing as well as taste good. Warm red wine is not refreshing. It doesn't even taste good.

White wines are almost always served chilled. A good rule of thumb is that the cheaper, or more precisely, the poorer the quality, the wine, the colder it should be served. Cold masks a lot of flaws. Conversely, cold will also mask a lot of the attributes you expect to find in that highly touted Chardonnay you spent big bucks on. A fine white wine should be served around 55 degrees Fahrenheit, in other words, cool, but not cold. Fifteen or twenty minutes in the refrigerator before serving should do the trick. A good quality white benefits from forty-five minutes to an hour of chilling.

What is true of white wine is also true of Champagne. High-priced, high-quality, *tete de cuvee* champagnes, like vintage Roederer Cristal, Krug Clos du Mesnil, and Dom Perignon simply do not strut their stuff when icy cold. Less expensive French champagnes and sparkling wines from places like Spain, Italy, and California, made with the same *methode champenoise* as the French versions, seem to taste better with a little more chilling than their very expensive counterparts. These are the wines you will find in the $20 to $60 price range for the French and in the $10 to $35 price range for the others. Serve these wines chilled, but not cold.

At the low end of the price scale are the jug wines that you find in 1.5-liter bottles costing under $10 and the bulk-process sparkling wines that you find for $3 a bottle or less in the discount houses and often at graduations and weddings. These sparkling wines taste better and better the closer they get to freezing. They also tend to be a bit sweeter, which makes them actually more enjoyable for most people on hot summer days than their pricier, but drier, counterparts. These sparklers are also especially suitable for mixing with cranberry or orange juice for punches or mimosas. In fact there is no reason whatsoever to use the more expensive stuff in these concoctions.

Quickly Chilling and Warming Wines

On many occasions you may want a bottle of white wine or champagne but do not have an hour or more to wait for it to cool its heels in the refrigerator while it reaches the appropriate temperature. Or perhaps it is a red wine that you stored in the garage in December and now suddenly decide, a month later, would be just the thing to go with that delicious Osso Buco you're preparing for dinner.

Here are a couple of quick fixes. White wine can be quickly chilled in the freezer of your refrigerator. A half an hour is usually enough. It sometimes happens a bottle is forgotten and left in the freezer overnight. The next morning when you discover the wine, it is frozen and the cork is pushed halfway out of the bottle. Surprisingly, this treatment does not seem to affect the wine adversely. Stand the bottle upright in the refrigerator and allow it to thaw before serving. It should be fine, but don't tell your guests what happened.

An even faster technique than the freezer is to fill a champagne bucket or any container that is at least three-quarters the height of the bottle and bigger around than the bottle. A plastic gallon container does the trick nicely. Fill the container one-third full with cold water and ice and place the bottle of wine in it. The water and ice mixture should come up at least to the shoulder of the bottle. Within ten minutes, the wine will be chilled. Within fifteen minutes it will be very cold. This technique works equally well and just as fast with larger amounts of wine and beer in larger containers such as ice chests. If you're having a party and don't want to fill up your refrigerator with wine bottles, this method is just the ticket.

Quickly warming wines, especially fine red wines is trickier. In fact, with an older red wine, our suggestion is to bite the bullet and just wait the two or three hours it may require for the wine to come up to 60 to 65 degrees Fahrenheit. Putting it on top of a stove that is turned on or a couple of feet away from a portable heater seems to work well. It will bring the wine up to the proper temperature in one-half to one hour, with little or no noticeable detrimental effects on the wine. With a young red wine, the only method we have found is to put it in a microwave set on defrost. The results, while not absolutely optimal, are reasonable. Just make sure you use the defrost setting. The other settings will cook the wine. Uncork the wine and set the microwave for three minutes. If after three minutes, the bottle of wine is still too cold, wait five minutes and then defrost it for no more than another three minutes, less if appropriate. Remember the wine will warm in the glass as well as in the bottle during the course of the meal.

Pairing Food and Wine

One often hears the expression, "It's a food wine." So what does this mean? The most obvious answer is that it goes well with food, which is true. Score one for the obvious. Why are some wines food wines and others not? For one thing, food wines have certain characteristics that allow them to be not only enjoyable with food but to play off the food, so that both the food and wine benefit from each other's company, a successful date, so to speak. Generally a good food wine has notice-able acidity, with an edge or crispness. It is not a highly extracted wine with a superabundance of fruit or oak flavors. Nor is it an overwhelm-ing wine in any one regard, but rather a wine in which the various components are in balance with each other.

Now don't get us wrong and think that we don't enjoy highly ex-tracted Zinfandels and Cabernets so bursting with fruit that you would imagine they might make a wonderful jam, or that we don't enjoy Chardonnays with butter and vanilla flavors as intense as a caramel sundae. These wines are best enjoyed by themselves, perhaps with a bite of cheese or some nuts, but when matched with a meal they often seem cloying and in competition with the food.

A wine that goes well with food is a wine that is enjoyable from the begining of the meal to end. One does not get tired or bored with it after a half a glass. It is a wine, which because of it's acidity, clears and refreshes the palate with each sip, so that the multiple flavors in the food are more accessible and enjoyable. Curiously, wines that are wonderful with foods don't do very well in medal competitions be-cause they are not wines that draw immediate attention to themselves.

Many people who love the bright fruit and intense flavors of Cali-fornia Cabernets might find Bordeaux wines made from the same grape rather boring. Yet the Bordeaux wines will more often pair with food better because they are not so intensely fruity and, perhaps, have more of an edge to them.

Match the Food with the Wine

One way to ensure that you get maximum enjoyment and value from your wine dollar is to try to match the food with the wine, or if you prefer, the wine with the food. The food you serve with a wine is almost as important as the temperature at which you serve the wine. A good pairing will enhance both. A mismatch can result in the wine tasting disappointing or even unpleasant.

Since rules are made to be broken, here's one that can be trashed on a regular basis. It's a favorite whipping boy of wine and food writers since there are so many exceptions to it. *Serve red wine with red meat and white wine with white meat, like fish, veal, or chicken breast.*

Despite the fact that this rule is as old-fashioned as Nehru jackets, it still has merit. It is easy to remember, and what's more, it's right more often than it's wrong, something you can't always say about your Internet stock picks.

Where this rule begins to be on shaky ground is when you bring such elements as sauces, spices, or rubs into the culinary picture. Aside from the fast food hamburger, chicken breast is the most popular entree item in America, so we'll start there. Following the rule spelled out above, chicken breast should be paired with a white wine. True or false? According to the rule, true. That's correct if the breast is simply roasted or grilled. What if we slather the chicken breast with a mild tomato-based barbecue sauce and grill it? In this case, you can probably serve it with a Chardonnay, Sauvignon Blanc, Zinfandel, or Pinot Noir. All will work. The barbecue sauce is not so dominant that it will overwhelm the chicken flavor or prohibit the pairing of the dish with a white wine, yet it still plays a significant enough role in altering the taste to make it possible to serve a red wine. Another possibility is to cook the chicken breast in a stew made with a red wine. Now the dominant flavor is the red wine sauce. A white wine can't compete. You need to serve the dish with a light- or medium-bodied red.

But what if you marinate the chicken in a Jamaican jerk rub with its hot peppers and exotic spices? Few wines pair well with this dish, but they do exist. Either a Johannesburg Riesling or a Gewürztraminer with their good acidity, floral flavors, and a touch of sweetness work well. These two wines also work well with a large number of ethnic cuisines such as Thai, Sechuan, Cajun, Mexican, Indian curries, in fact, with anything that is on the fiery side. Most wine drinkers do not like wines with any hint of sweetness, or think they don't. Somehow it has been planted in the American psyche that these wines are unsophisticated, something only winos and teenagers drink. This idea is unfortunate, because these wines, in combination with the right foods, are truly wonderful. So if you like spicy foods, give Riesling and Gewürztraminer a try. You'll be pleasantly surprised, if not downright dumbfounded by how good they can be. Another plus is that American-produced Gewürztraminers and Rieslings tend to be lower in alcohol as well as generally less expensive than Chardonnays and Sauvignon Blancs.

Red wines that often work well with spicy, highly flavored dishes are Pinot Noir, Syrah, and Zinfandel. In fact Pinot Noir is the most food-friendly wine, red or white, that there is, matching up nicely with a very broad range of dishes. The spice and pepper notes in Pinot Noir, Zinfandel, and many Syrahs allow them to work with foods possessing the same qualities, as well as red meat dishes of all persuasions. Cabernet Sauvignons on the other hand are not as versatile, though the tannins in them serve as a perfect foil to prime rib and roasts.

Most American Chardonnays on the market, with their heavy doses of malolactic fermentation and oak, are probably best as an aperitif, something to drink during the cocktail hour rather than with dinner. If you have a dish that cries out for a white wine, chances are that a Sauvignon Blanc or a Pinot Grigio will pair better with it than Chardonnay. Unfortunately there's a problem here. Most people simply like Chardonnay more than Sauvignon Blanc and probably haven't ever tried Pinot Grigio. They begin drinking Chardonnay before their meal and want to continue during their meal. If this descibes you, then by all means have Chardonnay with your dinner. It's your money, your palate, and your decision. It's not that big a deal anyway.

Perhaps we can formulate a rule with broader applications than red wine with red meat and white wine with white meat. *Select a wine to complement the dominant flavors in the dish: subtle with mild; bold with rich; slightly sweet or peppery with spicy or hot.* Of course, when your memory fails, or you're not sure, drink what you like.

One last thing regarding the pairing of wine and food. If the wine you're serving is one you've been saving for a special occasion, you should go to extra lengths to ensure that the food complements the wine. If you need help, turn to your wine merchant. These guys are really good. They appreciate fine food as much as fine wines and are a terrific source of information. Quite possibly they've tasted the wine you're planning to serve, perhaps with a meal at an excellent restaurant or at a special food and wine dinner they orchestrated somewhere, so they will be in a position to give you some great ideas for your menu.

Another invaluable source of information is the winery itself. Be sure to write, e-mail, or phone them well in advance of your dinner. Describe the wine you will be serving and ask for their suggestions. They will be able to offer some great ideas since they know the wine and have certainly tried it with a wide variety of foods. Besides, they have a vested interest in making sure their wine shines.

Some Tried and True Food and Wine Combinations

Certain food and wine combinations are so well established that they have almost become canons. Some examples are Chablis with fresh oysters, Champagne with caviar, red Bordeaux with roast prime rib, Burgundy with Coq au Vin, Port with Stilton cheese, Sauternes with foie gras.

Here are a few more worthy combinations:

Barbecued trout and Pinot Grigio
Poached salmon and mango salsa with Sauvignon Blanc
Poached salmon and hollandaise with Chardonnay
Barbecued salmon with Pinot Noir
Barbecued chicken with Chardonnay
Steak au Poivre with Zinfandel
Roast leg of lamb with Syrah
Roast turkey with Gewürztraminer
Honey-baked ham with Riesling
Artichoke fritata with Pinot Blanc
Grilled swordfish with Beaujolais
Thai salad with a Gewürztraminer from Alsace
Barbecued ribs with California Cabernet Sauvignon
Beef Wellington with Merlot
Roast loin of pork with a French Chenin Blanc
Pork and sauerkraut with a dry Gewürztraminer

Hamburgers with Zinfandel
Cracked crab with Champagne
Seafood and pasta in a tomato sauce with Sangiovese
Prawns sautéd in butter and garlic with Chardonnay
Grilled rack of lamb with Nebbiolo
Risotto and wild mushrooms with Pinot Gris
Oysters with Muscadet

Wine Glasses

Some of the attributes of wine that add to its enjoyment are visual: its color, its translucence, and the way it picks up and reflects light. Much or all of this is lost in colored or cloudy wine glasses.

An all-purpose wine glass should be as clear as possible. It should have a bowl shape with a smaller rim, to allow the wine to be swirled and to trap and concentrate the aromas and bouquet of the wine. It should have at least an eight-ounce capacity. This is your standard garden-variety good wine glass. But if you're really into ferreting out all the nuances and complexities a fine wine has to offer, then you might want to acquire some Riedel glasses. These are glasses for wine professionals, students of oenology, and wine geeks.

Riedel takes wine glasses into a whole new dimension, making a broad spectrum in different shapes and sizes, each designed to accentuate the characteristics of a particular kind of wine. The curious thing is that these glasses do work. The same wine tasted in one of Riedel's glasses that was designed for it will actually taste different than it will from a standard wine glass. Why? Because the design of the Riedel glass provides more olfactory information about the wine. Attributes are highlighted, flaws exposed. Warts no longer masquerade as beauty marks.

There are two categories of Riedel glasses, the Vinum and the Sommelier, both made from 24 percent lead crystal. The main difference between the series is the cost: the Vinum are machine made and cost $80 for six. The glasses in the Sommelier series are hand blown and retail for anywhere from $32 to $55 per stem, depending on the style of glass.

The real question is do you really care that much? Most people probably don't. Besides, most wines don't warrant the expense or the bother. However if you're looking for a little cache with your guests, you might want to have some Riedel glasses on hand for your next dinner.

Decanting Wine

Decanting wine is nothing more than pouring wine from one container into another. In the process, the wine is exposed to air. There are any number of reasons to do this, some of which follow:

- You have a beautiful crystal decanter you would like to serve the wine in.
- The original bottle is funky, with a torn or missing label or mold covering the bottle.
- It's a cheap wine and you don't want you guests to know what you're serving.
- You want your guests to try to guess the varietal or age of the wine but don't want to bring the bottle to the table in a brown paper bag.
- The cork or bits of it have fallen into the bottle.
- The wine has thrown sediment, and you don't want it to end up in the wine glasses.
- You want the wine to breathe so its aromas and flavors can expand before you serve it.

The first five reasons need no elaboration, but a few words about the last two may be in order. Older red wines throw sediment, a result of the tannins forming a chain that becomes so heavy that it falls out of solution to the bottom of the bottle. As the tannins drop out of the wine solution, the wine becomes softer and less bitter. The downside is that the sediment, if disturbed, can cloud the wine and make it taste gritty. To avoid this, you need to stand the bottle upright for a day or two before you serve it so that the sediment can settle to the bottom. Then you carefully decant it, the idea is to leave the heavier sediment behind in the original bottle.

In days gone by, people did this with a candle positioned behind the bottle so that as the sediment approached the neck of the bottle, they could see it and stop decanting. A steady hand and the nerves of a surgeon were considered to be prerequisites for this task. You've probably seen pictures of special baskets and cradles designed to aid the process. It's all part of the romance of wine for many connoisseurs: dark cellars, moldy old bottles of wine, and flickering candles. As charming and romantic as it is for some, for others it is just a bother.

Still, what do you do about the sediment? The easiest way to deal with it is to pour the wine through a funnel lined with an unbleached coffee filter into the decanter. What's so nice about this method is that neither candles nor a steady hand are necessary, plus none of the wine need remain behind. The technique works equally well when the corkscrew turns the cork into little pieces of bark, which, having nowhere else to go, drop into the wine.

The final reason on our list for decanting wine is that you want the wine to breathe so it can open up, an issue that puts a whole bunch of cowpokes on one side of the fence and a whole bunch on the other. Some critics maintain that decanting a wine, especially a young wine, doesn't benefit it. Others insist that it does. We think it does, sometimes. Why it makes a difference sometimes and not others, is mysterious. It's rarely detrimental to decant a wine, so no harm, no foul. We have found that good Cabernets with ten to twenty years of age can benefit enormously by being decanted a half hour before serving. The wine seems to blossom and come alive, while the same wine poured straight from the bottle will seem restrained and backward.

However we don't recommend decanting very old wines, which can fade quickly when exposed to aeration, though it's still often necessary to decant them because of sediment. Our recommendation is to open them and decant them immediately before serving. An old wine left in a decanter for half an hour before serving may have given up the ghost before you get to enjoy it.

Corks

Corks, along with glass bottles, are what make the aging of wine possible by providing a virtually airtight seal, thus preventing the wine from oxidizing or "going off" as the British say (though they never say where it goes off to, perhaps to a distant cousin in Yorkshire?). Corks are made from the bark of the cork tree, hence the name. While corks were certainly a high-tech, state-of-the-art invention when first introduced in the 1700s, time has disclosed that they are a less-than-perfect closure. Over time they dry out and decompose. Many of the first growth Bordeaux wineries recork bottles of their wines every twenty-five years or so because of this problem.

Another problem with corks has been that they were routinely bleached. This sometimes leads to the formation of a chemical compound called TCA, which contaminates the wine. Hence the term, the wine is "corked," which means in many cases the wine is so foul smelling that it is undrinkable. It is estimated that between 2 and 7 percent of wines are corked to some degree, depending on who is putting out the numbers.

Efforts to fix the problem have led to unbleached corks, which no one is quite sure has solved the problem, and to synthetic corks, composition corks, plastic corks, and screw tops. The last is used only for very inexpensive wines. The mystique and ritual of drawing a cork from a bottle of wine thwarts any change by the industry for a better closure. Ironically, with all the technical advances in winemaking over the last three centuries, we still get wine bottles stopped with something that often will not last as long as the beverage it's designed to protect, and with the added potential that it might totally ruin the wine. Still the idea that a $50 bottle of wine should have a screw top, no matter how effective, is anathema to the wine industry and to people who drink wine.

Corks are part of the heritage and romance of fine wine. Yet, if you were to open a bottle of wine that you spent half a week's pay on, only to find it corked and smelling like your trash can during a heat wave, you might wonder if corks are really all that romantic.

Saving Opened Wine

Often you open a bottle of wine, enjoy a glass or two, but don't want to drink any more. You're looking at half a bottle of wine or more, which if left out on the kitchen counter will go off by the following day. Since you paid anywhere from $5 to $100 for the wine, it seems a pity to pour down the drain what you don't drink right away. You would like, if possible, to drink it later. Fortunately you can do several things to retard or inhibit the process that causes the wine to go bad.

Wine is an organic substance and a food, just like apples, oranges, grapes, or potatoes. In the simplest terms, two things can cause food to go bad. Air, the stuff we breathe to stay alive, interacts with the food and causes it to change its chemical composition, in short, to decay or rot. The other major villain in this melodrama is heat. The hotter it is, the faster the process takes place. At low temperatures, the process is very slow, which is the reason that wines stored in those almost freezing cellars in the castles of Scotland taste much like they did when first bottled.

So with this rudimentary explanation of the process as background, you can choose various options to slow down as much as possible this degradation of your opened wine. The first option is to recork the bottle and put the remainder of the wine in a refrigerator. The colder it is, the longer it will take for the wine to go bad. If it's a white wine, and you plan to drink it the following day or two, the refrigerator will preserve the wine well enough. Same for a young red wine, just bring it out of the refrigerator a couple of hours before you plan to serve it, so it can come back to room temperature.

If you are not going to consume the opened wine within the next day or two, you will need to take further steps. Since air, or more specifically the oxygen in air, is what chemically reacts with the wine, the idea is to minimize the amount of air that comes into contact with the wine. The simplest, least costly, and most effective method, is to fill a smaller bottle with the remaining wine, seal it and put it into the refrigerator. You can keep a couple of empty 375-ml wine bottles around for just this reason. If you know you're going to drink only a couple of glasses of wine from a 750-ml bottle, after opening it, immediately fill a 375-ml bottle to the top with the wine, leaving just enough room for the cork, then seal it and put it into the refrigerator. This way the wine has minimal contact with air for the least amount of time. Red and white wines treated this way will remain fresh for weeks, even months. Nor does the container have to be a wine bottle.

A clean ketchup bottle with a screw top would be just fine, though it doesn't have quite the panache.

Two commercial methods of preserving left-over, opened wine are Private Preserve and a device called Vacu-Vin. Private Preserve is a cannister of inert gasses that are heavier than air. The gasses are under pressure, so you can squirt them into an open bottle of wine, where they will sink to the surface of the wine, forming a protective layer on top of the wine. Bottles of wine that have been gassed need to be stored upright. Over the years, we've gassed many bottles of wine with generally good results for up to several weeks. Saving wine beyond that time frame has always proved to be a bit iffy, though the manufacturer claims their product will preserve wine for six months or more.

Each cannister can preserve up to seventy-five bottles of wine and at around $10 a cannister, this works out to less than 8 cents a bottle. Eight cents to save $10 to $30 worth of wine is definitely a deal. It's also more convenient than pouring wine into smaller bottles, so you may find yourself actually using it more readily. You can find Private Preserve at most fine wine shops.

VacuVin is a small plastic pump that is used to extract the air from an opened bottle of wine, leaving a vacuum between the wine closure, which is a rubber stopper with a slit in it through which the air is sucked out, and the wine. When the pump is removed, the slit closes, providing a seal. We know several people who swear by it. We also know several who swear at it. We personally find the other two methods more convenient as well as more reliable.

The effectiveness of any technique is related to how long the wine has been open. The half bottle of wine that you poured directly from a 750-ml container to a 375-ml container immediately after opening is going to remain fresh and lively much longer than wine that has been left open at a dinner table for several hours before any attempts to preserve it have been made.

It is especially important that older wines be rebottled into a smaller container immediately after opening. Older wines that have been open for several hours already are well on their way over the hill. The oxidation process is too far along to be arrested or even slowed down much. So if you know beforehand that you won't be drinking the entire contents of the bottle, put what you won't consume into a smaller bottle right away or gas it and put it into the refrigerator. You'll find that it tastes just like the wine you drank when your first opened the bottle.

7

Collecting Wines

Wine is perhaps the only beverage capable of aging once it has been bottled. Coca-cola won't, beer won't, not even brandy will. Having made this assertion we should back up and explain what is meant by aging. *Aging is a process by which something evolves, changes, and becomes more complex over time. In short, it changes for the better.* However with wine, at a certain point, the changes that are occurring stop enhancing it, and the opposite happens. Hence we hear expressions like "The wine is going downhill," a phenomenon equally applicable to movie stars, athletes, and other public luminaries.

The ancient Romans are known to have liked aged wines. They would seal sweet red wines in amphora for fifteen to twenty years, then pop them open for a special occasion like a crucifixion or Gladiator Bowl XXV. With the fall of the Roman Empire and the subsequent arrival of the Huns to the very doorstep of Rome, leathers and wild animal skins replaced togas as fashion statements. It was the start of the "Dark Ages" for more than the garment industry. The aging of wines disappeared, possibly because the barbarians thought aging wines was something for effite intellectual snobs, but more likely because these forerunners of the Hell's Angels were party animals not given to waiting fifteen or twenty years for anything. Aging wines became a lost art, not to reappear until the 1700s when the availablity of glass bottles and corks to seal them made it possible to preserve wines from oxidation. The English with their cold castles and even colder dungeons, which could be easily converted to wine cellars, latched on to the idea of aging wine with enthusiasm. Besides, they had both the temperament, mumbling things like "quite a splendid bouquet, don't you agree," or "I hear Parker at the *Wine Tattler* thinks it might merit a 98 in another fifty years." At the time, the English also had the disposable income for such pursuits. In good vintages, they would buy wines by the cargo container, especially loading up on Ports and wines from Bordeaux, which they insisted on calling Claret, much to the annoyance of the Bordelais. Buying in volume most certainly enabled them to get terrific discounts, and, of course, the pound sterling was much stronger then.

Aside from understanding that wine is capable of aging, the most important thing to understand is that *most wines won't age or get better with time.* In fact, many more than most wines don't benefit from aging, more than 99 percent of them. In other words, *less than one percent of all the wines out there will improve with age.* If you're going to the trouble and expense of aging a wine, be sure it's a member of the 1 percent club. Considering the billions and billions of gallons of wine made every years, 1 percent still adds up to a lot of wine to select from.

Following is a list, though not exhaustive, and rife with exceptions, of the wines that will reward your patience as well as your investment of money and time. Of course, if you have more money than patience or time, you can purchase aged wines from merchants or auctions, though usually at a hefty premium. This premium, in the case of very rare and old wine can be as much as a thousand times the original cost of the wine. A little arithmetic will show you the financial viability of aging the wines yourself. Of course this assumes that you plan to be around to drink them when they're ready. For instance, the folks who purchased the 1961 first growth Bordeaux are still waiting. If they were in their forties at the time, they are in their eighties now. It's a tough call as to who's going to cross the finish line first, they or their wines. Fortunately, the way most wines are made today allows them to be consumed a lot sooner than their predecessors.

Wines That Will Reward Aging

Red Bordeaux, especially first, second, and third growths.
Italian Barolo, Barbaresco, Amarones, and the Super Tuscans.
Many California, Washington State, and Australian Cabernets, generally the more expensive ones. Later on we'll give you the names of some that are less expensive and are worth cellaring.
Many of the red wines from the Rhône Valley.
Syrahs.
The top Spanish wines from Rioja and Priorat.
Zinfandels grown in mountain vineyards.
Vintage port.
Sauternes.
Top red and white Burgundies from good vintages.
Vintage French Champagne.
German Spatlese, Auslese, Beerenauslese, and Trockenbeerenauslese.

These wines, under the proper storage conditions, can age anywhere from ten to more than one hundred years. However, there are no hard and fast guidelines to tell you when a particular wine is at its peak. Not only that, but one man's peak is another man's valley. Not uncommonly, a wine critic will proclaim that a particular wine still has years of evolution ahead of it, while another wine critic will offer her expert opinion that the exact same wine has gone into decline. Can they really be talking about the same wine, you wonder. If so, who's right? Actually, in a way they both are. For one critic, the wine has begun to develop the complexity and bottle bouquet that he or she looks for in an older wine. For the other critic, the wine has lost much of its fruit and has begun the downhill slide. For him, the wine has lost more than it has gained.

Ultimately, it should be your personal taste that determines when a wine is ready to drink. Fortunately, the aging of wine is not like a line on a graph that goes straight up, reaches a high point, and then drops straight down. What happens is that a wine will gradually improve over a number of years until it reaches a more or less level plateau where it will hang out for a while and then begin a gradual slide, ending up as not very good vinegar. For some wines, the time frame is ten or fifteen years, for others, the process is stretched out over more than a hundred. But the main point to remember is that the wine is evolving, changing, softening, and improving, becoming what the wine writer Michael Broadbent calls "harmonious." This is the glory and rationale for aging that small percent of wines that benefit from extended time in the bottle. This is what rewards your time, your money, and your patience. So *you* need to be the final arbiter of when the wine is ready.

Tannins and Acids: Who Needs Them?

The key components in red wines that enable them to age are tannins and acids. Together they give a wine its structure, much like framing gives a building its shape. Tannins are natural anti-oxidants that prolong the life of a wine. They help keep it from going over the hill before it has a chance to develop complexity and bouquet. Tannins are imparted to the wine from the skins and seeds, and to some extent from the wood barrels it is aged in. When the 1982 Château Pichon Lalande was first tasted out of barrel, some critics thought it lacked the necessary structure for greatness. Six months later, the oak barrels it was aged in had provided enough additional tannins to cause the same critics to radically upgrade their evaluation from a very good wine to a great wine.

The tannins in a young wine can impart an astringent or bitter taste and cause a severe case of dry mouth, like when your lips feel like they're stuck to your teeth. Over time, the tannins combine with one another and other phenols to form longer, more complex molecules. At a certain point, they become too heavy to remain in suspension and begin to drop out, like so many sixties' flower children. The wine begins to feel softer in the mouth and taste less bitter. However, while the tannins are combining and falling out of solution to the bottom of the bottle, the fruit is also fading. So in essence, what we have is a race. Will there be enough fruit left for the wine to still be enjoyable by the time the tannins are history? Usually yes, occasionally no. Trying to decide when can be a bit of a crap shoot, especially if you're unfamiliar with the particular wine. However, this is also part of the excitement and romance that comes with aged wines. When they are good, they are often very, very good, and when they're not, well, they're disappointing.

When a new vintage is tasted out of barrel, you will often read the various critics stating that the wines have either soft or hard tannins. In Bordeaux, 1982 was a vintage with soft tannins while 1986 was a vintage, especially in the Medoc, in which the tannins were considered to be hard. In the case of 1982 the fruit was so forward or ripe that many of the tannins were hidden by the rich fruit. The 1994 California Cabernets were rich ripe wines, enjoyable from day one. The 1995 Cabernets are less forward, less accessible, and considered to be more classical in style. So they need aging. Wines from vintages like Bordeaux's 1982 and California's 1994 are a pleasure to drink upon release and continue to be so for the rest of their lives. Yet they have the ability to age and develop complexity with time.

The 1986 Bordeaux will take time before they are ready to drink but will probably outlive the 1982s by quite a bit. The same can be said of the 1995 California Cabernets when compared with the 1994s. The problem with young tight-knit wines is that sometimes they do not evolve but remain tight and tannic until the fruit fades completely. They simply become old wines without style or charm, never having lived up to expectations.

Not every vintage can be a gangbuster vintage like 1982 in Bordeaux or 1994 in California. A problem that wineries have had to face is that most of their wines are consumed within a few years of release, regardless of whether they need to be aged or not. Not everyone has a cellar or is interested in laying down wine for years. This has led winemakers to try to make their wines more accessible upon release by finding ways to tame the tannins. Over the last ten years they have had quite a bit of success. They have come up with a number of techniques in the vineyard and in the cellar that have softened the edges of the tannin molecule, resulting in a gentler wine upon release.

Nowadays, you rarely need to wait a decade or more before you can drink a wine with pleasure. This in turn raises the question of whether or not these modified tannins will allow wines to age as long or develop quite the complexity as their predecessors did. Many winemakers feel they will. Others have reservations. Probably only time will resolve the question. For many wines it may be a moot point, since people will probably drink them before the wines have had a chance to age. Since you can drink many wines almost immediately after release, the question has changed from "How long do I have to age the wine before it is palatable?" to "Do I want to age it at all?"

Acidity is the other key element in determining whether a wine will age gracefully. It is what gives the wine its edge. Acid in the wine also helps keep it stable and prevents the growth of bacteria. A wine low in acidity will taste flat or "flabby" like many California Merlots, while a wine that is excessively high in acid will taste sour. Wines with an abundance of ripe fruit can have the requisite acidity, yet still taste almost sweet, because the fruit reduces the effects of the acidity on the taste buds. As a wine ages, it will lose some of its acidity. So a young, tannic wine with noticeable acidity will smooth out and become more pleasurable to drink as it ages. Generally, acidity in a wine will draw attention to itself only when it is too high or too low.

When purchasing wines to put away or age, you should select from very good or great vintages. If you have a finite amount of money, let alone a limited amount of space, it doesn't really make sense to buy lesser vintages. More often than not, a third or even fourth growth from a great vintage will far outshine a first growth from a mediocre vintage at a fraction of the cost. If you want to drink the wine over time, but don't want to wait ten or fifteen years before being able to enjoy the first bottle, choose wines from vintages the critics hail as "rich, bursting with fruit and with soft tannins." Avoid wines that are described with words like "tight," "closed in," or "tannic monsters." In fact it's not a bad idea to avoid such wines anyway.

Vintage charts are a quick and easy reference for getting a general handle on when a particular type of wine from a specific area might be ready to drink. With color coding denoting "hold," "ready to drink," and "whoops, too late," these charts are handy aids, especially if you are considering buying a wine with some years under its belt. Vintage charts are probably accurate somewhere between 70 to 80 percent of the time, so they beat flipping a coin or consulting a ouija board. You can request one from your local wine merchant.

Even better are publications like the *Wine Advocate*, the *Wine Enthusiast,* and the *Wine Spectator* that often do vertical tastings of different vintages and evaluate them. Thus if you own any of the wines that they review, you have a pretty good idea of how your wine might be doing, assuming that you stored it under favorable conditions. They also do horizontal tastings where they review, for instance, a large number of Cabernet Sauvignons or Bordeaux from a single year. Usually the protocol is to describe how each wine tastes now, and also to guess as to its future development.

Of course, if you have a case or two of a particular wine, you can always open a bottle every couple of years to see how it's progressing. Fine and good if you have that case of wine. If, however, you have only a bottle or two, you will have to rely on other people's opinions.

Perhaps the easiest way is also one of the best. Any good wine merchant, like the ones listed elsewhere in this book, have a number of people on staff who have a great breadth of expertise, who attend numerous tastings, and are likely to have the information you seek or know where to find it. Furthermore they are usually happy to share their knowledge with you in great detail. Just try to avoid getting into a lengthy conversation with them just before the holidays when their phones are ringing off the hook and they've been working fourteen-hour days.

Collecting Wines

What needs prompt people to be collectors? Most of us have collections, whether they are butterflies, jewelry, shoes, art, coins, toys, old 45 records, or beanie babies, as well as money. Collecting seems to be an almost primal need for many of us. Witness the relentless pursuit by an avid collector of a prized butterfly or an especially rare coin. That person becomes a hunter, tracking, stalking, moving in for the prize; but collectors are more than hunters. They are also organizers. Collections follow themes and years and styles. Even if the collection starts out on a random note, it soon finds its organizational thread, its unifying theme.

The people who collect wine are no different from their counterparts with their collections of Tiffany lamps or autographs of famous people. An inner need to possess more than one of a type is being met, while the need to hunt, to search, to organize is being satisfied. Yet collecting is not a survival mechanism. No one needs 147 porcelain cats or 13 Harley Davidson motorcycles or 5,000 bottles of wine. Collecting springs from some other well.

Of course, if you ask wine collectors why they collect wine, they will likely couch their motives in something close to survival. They will explain that if they had not bought that case of 1983 Palmer when it was released, they would not be able to afford even a single bottle at today's prices—and about this they are right.

There are many explanations, rationales, even excuses as to why people collect, yet each is only a fragment of the whole. Even if we added together all the reasons for collecting, we still might not completely understand why people collect the things they do. Yet we don't have to look far for, at least, a partial explanation that is hard to dispute. Collecting makes us happy. We feel like proud parents as our collection grows and improves. Collecting gives us a sense of satisfaction. It even gives us a sense of community.

We know that there are others just like us out there. Our friends and spouses may think we're nuts, foolish, even silly, but we know we are not alone. Others share the same passion, and we can talk to them. They understand, for they too are a little bit crazed, just like us. Start talking about a 1995 Screaming Eagle and their eyes do not glaze over, nor do they have to stifle a yawn, nor suddenly remember that they left their two-month-old child alone in the house. No, they are interested and give us validation. We share a bond with them that we do not share with others.

There are numerous other reasons for collecting wines besides the ones lying below the threshold. You might have an empty space in your home, that's well, empty. You think, why not fill it with wines before someone else fills it with old clothes or furniture? Besides, having a wine cellar or its equivalent has a certain cachet. You imagine saying to your dinner guests, "Be back in a minute. I'm going to pop down to the wine cellar to see if I can't dig up a bottle of 1961 Petrus to go with dinner." Or you imagine yourself talking with fellow oenophiles about a wine that was the star of a recent tasting in New York and casually mention that you think you might still have several bottles nestled in the corner of the cellar someplace. Wine cellars are the stuff of Walter

Mitty fantasies. This is perhaps one of their most important functions, and, of course, it's nice to have wine in them that you actually drink.

Another, less fantastical reason for collecting wines is that wines can increase substantially in value. Had you purchased, for instance, the 1982 Mouton Rothschild as a future in 1983, you would own a wine that is now worth nearly fifteen times what you paid for it, an increase of fifteen hundred percent. Pretty heady stuff when you think of it and certainly added incentive for collecting wine. Remember though, you don't want to mention how much your wine has appreciated when serving it at dinner, though something along the lines of "almost impossible wine to find nowadays, except at the Château" might be okay.

The Risks of Collecting Wine

Scams

If you are going to collect wines, you don't want to give validation to the expression "There's a sucker born every minute." While the actual odds are relatively small that the average wine consumer would fall victim to a scam, you should still be aware that they exist. Remember the dictums: *(1) Knowledge is your friend. (2) Partial knowledge is the same as no knowledge.*

Every so often, some financial publication will print a list of the top investments for the last ten years. During the seventies, gold coins headed the list. Unfortunately what many people did not realize was that the incredible returns reported were based on a very small number of very rare gold coins that had seen an outstanding run-up in price. Collectible gold coins as a whole fared nowhere near as well. Nonetheless, a number of coin dealers and boiler room operations started touting all gold coins as a surefire investment with possible returns as high as 1,000 percent to 2,000 percent within ten years. Needless to say, many people have been disappointed when the gold coins they bought failed to perform as touted, in fact, often failed to return even as much as a passbook savings account and in many instances lost money.

A similar situation developed with wine. A company came on the scene in the late 1980s that pitched the idea of investing in wine. The scenario was simple. Wine had seen an exciting appreciation in recent years. Examples were given of first growth Bordeaux and certain California Cabernets that had appreciated several hundred, even a thousand percent in a matter of a less than ten years. With this premise in mind, investors would put their money with the company who would buy wines, store them for their clients, and voila, in five to ten years the investors would be sitting pretty. The problem was that the wines the company purchased were not the wines that had seen the phenomenal price increases that had been used as the basis of their sales promotion. In fact they weren't even first tier investment wines. What's more, the wines they did purchase were often from mediocre or even poor vintages. Investors not only did not make money, but they lost money.

While we have not seen any similar wine-related investment opportunities in the past five years or so, it is possible that some variation on this theme will pop up sooner or later. Before parting with your money, talk the idea over with someone in the wine business for his or her take on the investment.

Counterfeit Wines

Counterfeit wines exist, though they seem to be limited primarily to older, very expensive wines, such as first growth Bordeaux and rare Burgundies. Generally what happens is that the bottle, for instance a 1947 Petrus, after it is emptied is then refilled with another wine with somewhat similar characteristics. If the cork has been carefully removed with the two-pronged Ah-So corkscrew, it can be reinserted into the bottle without the telltale holes that an ordinary corkscrew would make. A phony foil is made to cap the bottle and the bottle is sold again.

Given the improving quality of color copiers, it is possible that in the not-too-distant future, labels will be easily duplicated and this problem may become more widespread. Your best defense, even though it may not be totally foolproof, is to purchase such rare and expensive wines from merchants with unquestioned reputations who will stand behind the wines they sell. You may be able to find the wine for less at auction or on the Internet, but look at it this way, the extra cost serves as an insurance premium and provides peace of mind.

Buying From Private Parties on the Internet

Are the risks worth whatever savings you might realize? We don't think they are, as you have little or no recourse if the wine is flawed or not as represented.

Other Risks of Collecting

You might also reflect on other risks involved in collecting wine, none of which should deter you, but that you should simply be aware of. Wine is a perishable commodity. It does not withstand earthquakes or fires. Should your house be threatened by fire, you will not have time to rescue your collection because wine is heavy and cumbersome. Your insurance probably won't cover your losses, unless you have a special rider on your policy. Collecting wine can also cause maritial conflict, unless your partner shares your enthusiasm, which rarely seems the case. Generally, the significant other feels the money would be much better spent on redoing the garden, taking a trip to Maui, or investing in the stock market. You might find yourself driving around for several days with cases of wine in your car until you have the opportunity to slip them into the house without being seen.

Another calamity that can befall your wine collection is divorce. Since wine is community property, only half of it really belongs to you. Now, though you may not be interested in half of your partner's extensive necktie or teddy bear collection, be assured that your partner will be interested in half of your wine collection. Your spouse may have demeaned it, laughed at you, thought you silly when you were acquiring it, but when it comes time to go separate ways, your spouse and your spouse's lawyer will see the collection as another asset to be split. Faced with the prospect of having to give up half of your pride and joy, you may find yourself drinking far more than you normally would.

Another downside to having a wine collection is that some of your wines will go bad. A case of wine you planned to drink over four or five years gets hidden by accident. By the time you rediscover it, it's vinegar. But this is minor concern, for the converse is equally true. It may be great. Life's a bit of a gamble, and to some extent, so is a wine collection. This is actually part of its charm. If you want certainty, collect U.S. Treasury bonds.

Although there is no special age at which people begin to collect wine, the collecting urge seems to come over most people in their late thirties and early forties. Perhaps a biological clock kicks in. Perhaps it's a matter of disposable income, perhaps a combination of the two. Whatever it is, you've reached the stage, and you've decided you enjoy wine. You might even read about the stuff in the wine columns in your local paper. Maybe you even subscribe to the *Wine Spectator* or the *Wine Enthusiast*. Maybe someone has given you a case of French Bordeaux as a Christmas gift. Whatever the reasons, you make the decision to start a wine collection.

It really doesn't matter what wines you collect. As with all collections, in time yours will find its theme, its own logic. One thing you must understand: You have a finite amount of space, be it a small closet or a cellar capable of holding several thousand bottles. At some point the space will fill up. It happens to every collector, so you must be judicious in the wines you put into the space.

What Wines Not to Collect

Since you may be just starting out, the most important thing to understand is that *most wines do not improve in the bottle.* In fact, less than ½ of 1 percent of all wines get any better, so the only reason to buy large quantities of most wines is because you got a great deal on them and plan to drink them in the next couple of months or years. Put these wines in the garage. They'll probably be okay there. If your garage is cluttered, remember where you put the wines because they have a limited lifetime. Save the space in your cellar or insulated closet for wines that actually get better with time. Buy wines for everyday drinking on an as-needed basis.

Where to Store Your Wines

If you live in a small apartment and every bit of space is being used, there are several other places that might be suitable for your wine collection. One is with friends or relatives. If they don't drink wine, this is a definite plus. Mothers usually respond warmly to having grown children store wines in their homes, because those children will visit much more often. Rental storage lockers are also a viable option. Ask for a storage space on the ground floor, far from the outside walls, in the middle of the first floor. This location will be insulated from outside temperatures by other lockers. Begin your search in the middle of summer when the temperature is hottest. If where your locker is located is still cool, you know your wines will be fine. Rentals for a closet-sized space in which you can store forty to fifty cases of wine is usually quite reasonable if you sign on for any length of time. Be sure to get a very good lock for the door to your storage space.

A third alternative is storage lockers that are designed for the storage of wine. These are temperature controlled and are a lot more expensive than Mom's basement or a general storage facility, though not necessarily better. The downside to storing wines away from home is that you have to go get them, often at hours that are not convenient for you, that and the extra money it costs you. They do, however, allow you to have a place for your growing wine collection. Storage lockers are also a good alternative when your wine collection starts overflowing your in-home storage capacity or your spouse puts a foot down and says, "Enough already. No more wine."

Storage Conditions: Some Elemental Facts

What is true about storing your wines away from home is also true about storing wines in your own house. You need to find a spot that is cool year round, without extreme temperature fluctuations, and that is secure from teenage sons and their friends. This eliminates the spot next to the furnace or the hot water heater. It also eliminates the attic unless it is very well insulated. The spot you select does not have to be perfect, but it can't get hot for more than brief periods of time or too damp. Cold, wet basement storage causes mold to grow on the bottles and ultimately destroys the labels. It also causes the cardboard boxes to grow weak and fall apart.

We've read about a wine collector who stored his wines in his garage where in the summer in the late afternoon the temperature would reach into the 90s. However, every evening he would open the garage doors and let the cool night air in. Because the wines were in their original cardboard cases and were stacked together, the insulation provided by the cardboard was adequate to keep the wines in good shape. This solution though not optimum was adequate since it generally takes more than one day of high temperature to bring the temperature of a case of wine to a point where it might be detrimental.

Wine racks in the living room, while attractive, really shouldn't be used for wines you do not intend to consume within the next couple of months because the average living room is often between 70 and 75 degrees. The ideal temperature for wine storage is between 55 and 60 degrees Fahrenheit. At this temperature the wines evolve slowly and gracefully. When wine critics talk about a wine lasting fifteen years before starting downhill, they are assuming that it will have been stored between 55 and 60 degrees. Wines that are stored at higher temperatures will age more quickly. This may not be such a bad thing if you don't have the thirty or more years some wines require before they are ready to drink.

On the other hand, if the wine is stored at too high a temperature it may not develop those flavor characteristics or complexity one hopes for from an older wine. It may taste clunky, disjointed, and disappointing. However if a wine is stored at too low a temperature, its evolution will be glacial. Witness the nineteenth century Bordeaux that were stored in the basements of Scottish castles where the temperatures were in the low 40s. The wines were still youthful a hundred years later, though the original owners certainly weren't.

There are several books about building a wine cellar that can be helpful if you want to go the elaborate route, with temperature-controlled rooms and so forth. If you live in an apartment and want a more sophisticated approach to wine storage than a spare closet, you might look into the variety of temperature-controlled units currently on the market. These have come a long way since their early days and are now available in a variety of furniture styles and capacities. But they are expensive and don't really do a much better job than a well-insulated closet or storage space, though they do look spiffy and call immediate attention to your wine collection. In the back pages of the

Wine Spectator you will find literally dozens of companies who will be happy to sell you one of these temperature- and humidity-controlled units for your wine collection.

What Wines Are Worth Collecting?

When we talk about collectible wines, we are not dismissing the other 99.5 percent of wines as insignificant or somehow inferior. They are simply wines that will not improve with extra time in the bottle. These are wines that taste their best when they are purchased.

With every rule, every injunction, there are always exceptions. If you really like certain wines that you know sell out within weeks or months of release, by all means buy them and store them but don't forget to drink them. Many of the more expensive Zinfandels like Ridge Lytton Springs or Geyserville, Rafanelli, and Saddleback Cellars fall into this category. Spectacular upon release, these wines are filled with an abundance of exuberant fruit. However, they rarely, if ever, get better over time. Instead they begin to fade within a few years to a shadow of their former selves. If you want to drink these wines, you have to buy them, and you have to store them. But remember to drink them within a few years.

So what wines fall into the *collectible* category? Perhaps it is best to approach this question from the other end of the horse and ask what wines are not collectible. Baldly stated, very few white wines have the ability to improve with age or in value, including probably 99.7 percent of all Chardonnays, Sauvignon Blancs, Gewürztraminers and the less-well-known French, Italian, and Spanish white varietals. These wines are best drunk young.

The proportion of reds that are not worth collecting is almost as high. If you want to fill your cellar with jug wine, do so. It's your money, your cellar, and in reality you have to satisfy only one person. If it makes you happy, do it. However, the odds are pretty good that you are a person who not only enjoys wine, but also gets a rush from knowing that the wines in your cellar are going to be worth more to-morrow than they were yesterday. If you were to walk into your wine merchant's shop five years from now, you would find that the wines you bought for $15 a bottle are now selling for $30 to $40. Given the way prices are spiraling upward for collectible wines, this might be a modest appreciation.

Even though less than ½ of 1 percent of all wines produced warrant collecting, you still have an awesome amount of wine to select from. Dozens of varieties, thousands and thousands of wineries and vintages reaching back over a hundred years, all add up to a lot of wine and a lot of choices.

In this section we will attempt to simplify the selection process for you, help you make intelligent choices, and justify the price of this book. *Basically there are two reasons to collect wines.* You want the wines and they will not always be available. So you buy them to be sure you have them. The other reason is that if you don't buy them now, they will cost substantially more at some future point in time. These are the rational reasons. However, we do not always do things for strictly rational reasons, though we tend to justify our actions in such terms. In actuality, there are numerous other reasons why people collect wine. And no two collectors are identical, even those who collect the same wines, so it is important to recognize your uniqueness and to understand what motivates your decisions. Whether you are just getting started collecting wine or already have ten thousand bottles in your cellar you need to know and understand what guides your buying decisions. Are you an impulse buyer? Does a good review of wine send you scrambling for the phone to try to lock up a couple of cases of the wine? Do the opinions of wine-knowledgeable friends sway your decision? Is there an intoxicating rush from securing wines that you know your friends were unable to procure? Do you get a warm, fuzzy feeling after buying a couple of cases of great wine? Do you just like a certain kind of wine and want it in your cellar? Do you taste extensively and then make your decisions? Are you a sucker for a good buy, even if you're not crazy about the wine? Do you buy wine because it has prestige and an aura surrounding it? These are just a few of the reasons people buy wine. There are many more.

The point in trying to understand your motivations is to realize that some are rational and some aren't. Curiously, the irrational ones are usually the ones that are the most compelling and satisfying. If you can get a handle on what prompts you to buy what you do, you can avoid the mistakes wine collectors often make: buying too much of a certain kind of wine, buying wines you may not actually like, or buying because someone else thinks they're terrific and recommends them, or even because your wine-collecting friends are buying them.

There are several advantages to approaching your wine buying from both pleasure and financial perspectives. Besides having a store of wines you personally like, you have wines that will increase in value. If your tastes change, at least the wines in your collection can be traded or sold. If you get swept up in *buying fever* and buy far more of a certain wine than you can ever expect to consume, you will not be stuck with it and find yourself drinking $50 bottles of wine at the back-yard barbecue.

There is a tendency to get caught up in the romance of wine, yet basically, wine is a commodity, just like pork bellies. It can be bought, sold, traded, or given away. And *like all commodities, the laws of supply and demand play the key role*. Just because you like a wine doesn't mean everyone else will. What is also equally true is just because you don't like a particular wine doesn't mean there aren't thousands of other people who will pay ridiculous prices for it. Your personal tastes will only dictate one thing: how much you will pay for a bottle of wine. Not how much someone else is willing to pay.

You should have no difficulty finding wines you like that will age. If you don't care whether the wines in your cellar will be worth more in five or ten years, you are unique, lucky, and psychologically well adjusted, and probably have had a much better childhood than the rest of us. However, most people get a great sense of satisfaction knowing that the wines in their collection not only taste great but also are worth a bunch more money than what they paid for them.

The Most Collectible Wines in the World: Bordeaux

The most collectible wines in the world are from the Bordeaux region in France, and they have been for centuries. Thomas Jefferson and Ben Franklin were fans and collectors of these wines. Years ago, Michael Broadbent, who is the director of wine for Christies auction house, detailed in a little book called *The Compleat Winetaster and Cellarman* a list of wines worth buying and laying down. "By and large, only the top wines from major districts will improve with age in bottle, indeed need to be kept to achieve full maturity." He goes on to point out that Claret from the leading châteaux and from the better vintages heads the list. Of the more than four hundred wines from Bordeaux, he felt that only a hundred or so developed interestingly over a ten- to twenty-year period and "only twenty to thirty chateaux have a universal reputation and are worthy of investment." Originally published in 1968, the advice is still valid today. Simplified even more, we can state: *First growth Bordeaux from outstanding vintages have consistently and significantly increased in value over time.*

Numerous other wines are good investments. Some might increase in value more than others, but probably none are as consistent or reliable as the first growth Bordeaux. These are wines with a record for quality and price appreciation going back over hundreds of years.

It is very important that you remember the part of the statement that says *from outstanding vintages.* Wines from mediocre or just good vintages rarely become great and rarely appreciate enough to justify buying them as an investment, though the wine trade will hype so-so vintages with the same enthusiasm that they sell the great vintages. After all, they have merchandise to sell, mortgages to pay, and kids to send to college.

There is a major problem with buying first growth Bordeaux wines. They have become absurdly expensive. To give you an idea how much prices for them have escalated in fifteen years, understand that in 1983 futures for most of the first growths from the 1982 vintage were selling for $350 a case, and upon release the wines sold for about $500 a case, not inexpensive, but still affordable. Futures for the 1995 vintage of the same wines were eight to ten times more than the 1982s cost. The year 1995, like 1982, was an outstanding vintage. What is interesting is that the two following vintages, 1996 and 1997 were much less so, yet the prices for the wines as futures continued to climb. People who bought the 1995s have already seen substantial increases in the value of their wines. This has not been the case with the 1996s and 1997s. Those who purchased these vintages will wait a lot longer to see any upward price movement, especially since the 2000 vintage is being hailed as one of the best of the last half century and will certainly attract most of the interest and money, even though the prices will be the highest ever. *Vintage is critical.*

The Importance of a Well-Established Track Record

Another key factor in determining the ultimate collectability of a wine is its track record. How long has it been around? Do people know how the wine will evolve over time? Is it predictable? Wines from new wineries are unknown quantities. The wines may taste great now, but will they taste even better in ten or fifteen years? Do they justify the investment in both time and money? Often they do. Sometimes they don't. With Bordeaux, you have track records measured in centuries, not years.

The track record of a wine is also key to determining the size of the market for any given wine. New wines have not had an opportunity to develop a following like the older wines have. California Cabernets can outshine their Bordeaux first growth counterparts in blind tastings, yet the built-in demand for first growths keep their prices approximately 300 percent higher than their New World brethren. Will California Cabernets someday catch up in release price with the first growth Bordeaux? Maybe, but not for at least another ten or twenty years. Are select California Cabernets then likely to see a spurt in their value? Are they a good investment for these reasons? Probably they are. No one knows for sure, but the likelihood of a narrowing gap in prices between first growth Bordeaux and the best California Cabernets is good. One reason is the phenomenal run-up at auction in the prices of some of California's superboutique Cabernet Sauvignons, wines that have increased by as many as fifteen times their original release price of $75 to $100.

Price Escalation in the Last Ten years

Fifteen years ago, no one could have predicted the prices premium wines are commanding today. A combination of affluence, demand, and scarcity have propelled prices for top wines through the threshhold of reason. As the general world population increases in size and has greater disposable income to spend on luxury items, the demand will continue to outstrip supply. The great red wine vineyards of Bordeaux, Burgundy, and California have hit their production ceilings. Year in, year out, the great vineyards produce more or less the same amount. Some years when conditions are ideal, quantity rises above the norm, but not by much. As a result, prices will continue to climb. Finite quantity plus increased demand results in increased prices, just as in Adam Smith's day.

Just how much the role of scarcity combined with feverish demand can propel the price of wine is illustrated by the California Cabernet Sauvignon from Screaming Eagle. From a small vineyard site, the winery produces approximately four hundred cases of wine each year. Each year the wine receives lavish praise from the wine press, but because of its minuscule production few people have the opportunity to purchase the wine. Sold almost exclusively from the winery to restaurants and to people on its mailing list, the wine is unavailable to the general public. If you're not on the mailing list, about the only way you can purchase the wine is at auction, where the wine sets record after record for California Cabernets. A case of the 1994 Cabernet Sauvignon released at less than a $100 a bottle, sold at auction for $10,600. This is a price increase of over 1,000 percent, an example of prices going from the ridiculous to the absurd.

The scarcity factor also plays a major role in high prices of older vintages of wine. Much of the wine from great vintages like 1929, 1945, 1947, 1959, and 1961 has already been consumed. Those bottles that remain command prices often hundreds, sometimes thousands, of times more than the original cost of the wine.

Are Fine Wines a Good Investment?

You may well ask, "Just how good an investment is fine wine?" If the collector acquires his wines carefully, stores them properly, and sells them at a propitious moment, they are a very good investment. Like all commodities, they have their ups and downs. The 1982 first growths saw a remarkable run-up in value through 1997 when, for instance, Mouton Rothschild was commanding up to $7,500 a case at auction, almost twenty times its cost as a future. In 1997 the price began to slide, dropping to below $5,000 a case. The return was still healthy, if not quite so heady as when it was at its top. Will the 1982s stage a return to their top prices and continue to increase in value? Recent auction results show a return to form for the first growths, with Mouton Rothschild fetching better than $7,000 a case. Will they continue to climb? The answer is yes, but how fast is any one's guess. Might they fall again? Possibly.

Many factors come into play in determining the price of these wines. One of the reasons for the steep run-up in price of Bordeaux was the entrance of wealthy consumers from the Pacific Rim countries. Flush with cash, they became serious buyers of first and second growths in a big way. As is the case with any commodity of which there is a finite supply, this increased demand forced prices up. Yet with the Asian economies in turmoil and not likely to recover for some time, the prices, after dipping 40 percent, have returned to previous levels. Other buyers from other countries have taken up the slack.

There Are Better Investments Than Wine

Although wines are a very good investment, certainly better than gold has been for the last fifteen or twenty years, wines are not as good an investment as, for instance, stocks. First of all, they pose problems of storage and risk from natural disaster like fire and hurricanes. Very few wines come close to the spectacular run-up in value of stocks like Intel or Microsoft. If one is looking for a pure investment, one that can be sold with a phone call in a matter of a few minutes and for which there is a very large market, stocks outshine wines easily. However, if you like wines, like collecting, and like the idea of what you own appreciating in value, then collecting wines can be a pleasant hobby and a good investment.

Wines certainly have a more romantic aura surrounding them than shares of a stock. If your wines do not appreciate, you will always be able to drink them, which is some consolation and is certainly more than can be said of a stock pick that tanks.

After hearing the case for first growth Bordeaux as being the best wine investment around, you might need to look elsewhere unless you are willing to pay $6,000 to $10,000 per case for the 2000 vintage. However, plenty of opportunities exist, though without quite the surety of the first growths for price appreciation, but these opportunities can be a lot more exciting and fun without the exhorbitant price tag. Except for the very rich, only the most avid of wine buffs can open a $500 bottle of wine without a sense of conflict and trepidation.

Other Collectible Bordeaux

The Bordeaux hierarchy of wines was established in 1855 by the simple expedient of classifying the wines by their purchase price at the time. This classification lists the first growths, the second growths, the third growths, the fourth growths, the fifth growths, and the Cru bourgeois [common growths] estates, in all, adding up to hundreds of wineries. For collecting purposes, we are going to follow Broadbent's advice and focus on certain wines from the second growths and some of the third growths that merit investment (for more information on the Bordeaux classification, see the glossary at the end of this book).

One second growth, Leovilles Las Cases, has established an outstanding reputation over the last fifteen to twenty years with wines that matched or surpassed the best of the first growths. The owner decided that since his wines were so good, why not charge the same as the big boys. So he doubled the price for the 1995 vintage to bring it in line with prices being fetched for the first growths. And he has been getting it—supply and demand.

So what's left that might be considered relative bargains? There is:

Pichon Lalande
Cos d'Estournel
Figeac
Gruaud-Larose
Beychevelle
Ducru-Beaucaillou
La Lagune
La Mission Haut-Brion
Pichon Baron
Montrose
Palmer
Calon-Sègur
Evangile
Talbot
Lynch-Bages
Canon
Pavie

Though not inexpensive, they are good values, especially when the price-quality ratio is compared with the first growths. At certain times these wines will outshine most of their first growth brothers, for instance, the 1961 Palmer and the 1982 Pichon Lalande. What we said about the vintage being important for the first growths is just as important with these wines. Great wines are generally only made in great years, but not all the wines from a great vintage will necessarily be great or even good, especially in Bordeaux. So how does one find out which wines from a particular vintage are worth buying and which ones are not? *Research:* There are numerous tools available to the consumer in the form of magazines, reviews from wine merchants, and wine newsletters. All have information, but some have more than others. *The Single Most Valuable Source of Information on Current and Recent Vintages from Bordeaux is the* Wine Advocate.

The Wine Advocate

Robert Parker was an attorney who, in the early eighties, began publishing a newsletter reviewing fine wines. The year 1982 was a watershed vintage for Bordeaux wines and the *Wine Advocate*. Bordeaux had not had a truly successful vintage since the early sixties, while Parker was struggling to establish his newsletter. In 1983 he traveled to Bordeaux to taste the unreleased wines from the barrel. He proclaimed it a great vintage, perhaps the finest since 1961. Many of the Bordeaux producers agreed with him, though few other wine critics or writers did. He must have felt as if he was a voice crying in the wilderness. Other writers found the wines from the vintage too ripe, not classic, or not age-worthy.

Parker defended his evaluation, noting similarities between the 1982 and 1947 vintage, which was still drinking spectacularly. Plus subscribers to his newsletter had an unequivocal numerical score as a point of reference as to precisely how Parker evaluated a wine. A second growth wine receiving a 98 was better than a first growth wine with a 93. Scoring eliminated much of the mystique surrounding wines and simplified decision making. Consumers who had never bought French wines felt confident in their choices.

Readers who followed his advice were able to purchase first and second growth Bordeaux at what must seem like fire-sale prices today, Mouton Rothschild at $350 a case, Pichon Lalande at $110 a case, Leoville-Las Cases at $115 a case and so on. To put these prices in perspective, a single bottle of 1995 Leoville-Las Cases costs close to $300 dollars now versus the less than $10 one would have paid for the 1982.

The spectacular quality of the 1982 vintage became apparent as Château after Château and critic after critic lined up to proclaim its quality. Parker's reputation was firmly established. Xeroxed copies of his newsletter were passed from wine lover to wine lover who hurried to secure cases of the 1982s he had written so highly of. The subscriber base for the *Wine Advocate* quickly doubled and doubled again. Bordeaux, long the wine of the upper classes and the rich, was suddenly being bought by scores of middle-class Americans who had a reliable guide to the mysteries of French wine.

While Parker in not infallible, he's been right much more often than not. Nor does he hide from his mistakes or refuse to change his opinion. Originally he gave the 1982 Pichon Lalande a score in the high 80s after tasting it out of the barrel, feeling it did not have the necessary tannins to give it structure. After the wine was bottled, and he had a chance to taste it again, he revised his score radically, giving it a 98. The wine had acquired the necessary structure from its time spent in oak barrels. And when a wine that he has given consistently high scores to comes up short, he does not gloss over its failings. He may have favorites, but they do not affect his critical judgment. He is not always right, but he does have the courage to be honest with himself and with his readers. Combined with his prodigious memory and excellent palate, his evaluations have become the Bible for serious wine consumers. Such is Parker's influence that every year the major châteaux in Bordeaux await his evaluations of the current vintage, and often set prices accordingly.

Parker's Track Record

You can see how accurate Parker's evaluations have been by looking at the prices commanded by the wines he had initially given high ratings to. Few have failed to multiply in value many times over, out-distancing the other wines of the vintage in the same classification in price and desirability. If you look at the wines from the first and second growths of Bordeaux that he has rated above 90 points, you can see that they have invariably increased in price.

But we are forced to wonder sometimes if this might not be a case of the tail wagging the dog. That is, if Parker gives a wine a high score, it follows that it will automatically become desirable. So isn't it simply a matter of a wine's rise in price being a direct consequence of what Parker thinks of it, not its inherent quality? It is an interesting hypothesis, and there may be a vestige of truth in the idea, but not much. Most of the first growth Bordeaux produce around twenty-five thousand cases of wine a year. Many people, critics included, will have the opportunity to taste these wines. If the score is high and the quality is not commensurate with it, the wine, like the emperor's new clothes, will be seen for what it really is. The ultimate determination of a wine's price, the marketplace, will value it accordingly. However, we can't think of any first or second growth Bordeaux that Parker has rated highly that have not increased considerably in price.

Nevertheless, the correlation between a high score and an increase in price may or may not hold true for other wines. For instance, he has rated many California Zinfandels highly, but they have not appreciated for several reasons, one of which is that few Zinfandels improve with bottle age. In fact, just the opposite is true. So just because he gives a wine a high rating, does not guarantee it will increase in value. We're sure Parker will adamantly maintain that he is not in the business of predicting which wines will gain in value. That many of his highly rated wines do so is dependent on many factors; the score he accords a wine is just one.

Besides Parker's comprehensive evaluation of each Bordeaux vintage, he and his very qualified assistant/associate Paul Roveni also taste and rate thousands of other wines from all over France and the world.

Other Publications That Offer a Critical Evaluation of Collectible Bordeaux

The *Wine Spectator*

The second most influential wine publication in the United States regarding first and second growth Bordeaux is the *Wine Spectator*. Like the *Wine Advocate*, it evaluates each vintage of Bordeaux from barrel tastings. Because it publishes every two weeks it is more likely to be the first publication out with an evaluation of the previous year's Bordeaux vintage. Like the *Wine Advocate*, it gives both a descriptive evaluation of each wine as well as a numerical score. The first scores fall within a 5 point range, such as 95–100, 90–95. Later, the wines are tasted after bottling and a more precise score is awarded.

It is interesting and certainly worth noting that the *Wine Advocate* and the *Wine Spectator* do not always agree, especially when they present the overall merits of a vintage. The *Wine Spectator* was much more enthusiastic about the 1985 vintage than Parker was. The following year Parker was enthusiastic about the 1986 vintage, especially the first and second growths from the Médoc region of Bordeaux, while the *Wine Spectator* was less so. In the simplest of terms, if you had purchased the *Wine Spectator's* top recommendations in 1985 and Parker's top recommendations for 1986, you would see your wines from 1986 rise in price more than the wines from 1985. Is this simply a case of Parker being more influential than the *Wine Spectator*? We don't think so, but it doesn't really matter. Remember, the race is not always to the swift nor the battle to the strong, but you're more likely to win if you bet that way. However, when the two publications agree a wine is outstanding, you can be pretty certain that you have a slam dunk.

The *Wine Enthusiast*

The *Wine Enthusiast* is one of the three most widely read wine publications, along with the *Wine Spectator* and the *Wine Advocate*. Evaluation of the latest Bordeaux vintage is based on barrel tasting and, while a reliable guide to the quality of the vintage, it lacks the comprehensiveness of the other two publications.

Other Sources of Information

There are a number of other sources of information, magazines like the British publication *Decantor* and small-circulation wine newsletters, all of which are fun to read and have merit and competence to varying degrees but which we don't particularly recommend when it comes to selecting Bordeaux that you expect to gain in value. But if you are looking for wines that have not been reviewed by either the *Wine Spectator* or the *Wine Advocate* and that might prove to be great values for personal drinking, you just might discover some gems.

The same holds true with reviews of the vintage that the large wine merchants put in their monthly newsletters for their customers. Their evaluations may be spot on or not, but this is definitely a case of consumer beware. Unlike the magazines and the independent newsletters, they are in the business of selling you wine in which they have taken positions, so one should take their remarks with a grain of salt.

Wine Futures

Buying Bordeaux Futures

Futures are wines that are sold several years before they are to be released. So even though you technically own the wine, you will not be able to take actual possession of it for another two years. There are basically two rational reasons for buying futures, in addition to any number of other reasons.

The first reason is: The wine you want to buy is offered at a discount to its release price. The Bordeaux châteaux offer their wines in a series of releases or *tranches* (slices) with the price usually increasing with each successive *tranche.* This sales technique is the wineries' way of judging demand for their wines and making sure that they do not sell them either too cheaply or too quickly. A given wine, for instance, Château Margaux, is at its least expensive when the winery makes its first futures offering. If the first *tranche* sells out quickly, the Château raises its price for the next *tranche*, so the price to the consumer goes up. Price increases are particularly likely in exceptional years when demand from collectors is heavy. In less hyped vintages, the price increases will be minimal. *These wines from lesser vintages will find their way into the market at close to the initial price; therefore, they don't warrant the price as futures.* Basically, what consumers have done is loaned their money to the winery for two years without gaining any interest or appreciation.

Should a wine receive a score of 98 or higher, the winery is well aware that it will enjoy a tremendous demand for its wine and set its first release price accordingly.

The second reason is: Because you want to be sure of getting some. The wine may be your favorite, and you might want to ensure that you will be able to get some. Or the wine may be highly coveted by other wine collectors after receiving glowing reviews. Or maybe the wine has a limited production, several hundred to several thousand cases, and might not be available later on. It makes sense that you will buy it as a future to lock in the amount you want.

California Futures

Until recently, a number of California's wineries sold futures of their top-of-the-line Cabernet Sauvignons at significant discounts from their release prices. They did not follow the French system of releasing the wines in successive *tranches*. Instead, they released a given amount of the year's production as a future offering, and when that sold out, they no longer sold the wine until its actual release several years later. However, with prices for their wines escalating greatly year after year, many wineries have discontinued this practice, fearful of selling their wines too cheaply. Now in California, only two wines are offered as futures, the Robert Mondavi Reserve Cabernet and the Ridge Monte Bello Cabernet Sauvignon. Curiously, now that so many wineries have discontinued the practice, Château Montelena, which never sold its wines as futures, has decided to do so, but it will follow the French practice of releasing its estate Cabernet Sauvignons in *tranches*, raising the price with each successive offering, in this way hoping to avoid selling their wines at less than the market will bear. Perhaps other California wineries who had stopped offering their wines as futures will begin again under the *tranche* system.

While only a few top-of-the-line Cabernet Sauvignons are offered for sale in California, one store in Washington, D.C., MacArthur Liquors, offers twenty or so California Cabs on a futures basis. So if you're interested in buying futures, it behooves you to get on their list.

MacArthur Liquors
4877 MacArthur Blvd., N.W.
Washington, D.C. 20007
202-338-1433
www. bassins.com

Do California Cabernet Sauvignons Warrant Collecting for Investment Reasons?

The answer is yes! The best ones do. Though you should be aware that the top California Cabernet Sauvignons do not have the world-wide collector base nor the lengthy track record that the French Bordeaux have, so they have not seen the same price appreciation as their counterparts. However, with the price of older Bordeaux out of the range of many collectors, interest in older California vintage Cabernet Sauvignons has begun to heat up, and prices at auction have started to rise. How high and where they will plateau is anyone's guess, though it is doubtful they will match the prices for first and second growth Bordeaux, with the exception of small-production wines like Screaming Eagle and Colgin that have attained a cult-like status, and for which there seems to be no ceiling.

Where to Buy Bordeaux Futures

Numerous wine shops and retailers offer wine futures. If you are interested in buying futures, be sure to get on their mailing lists. There are often significant differences in price between what each of the retailers sells a given wine for, so *it is wise to comparison shop.*

Here is a list of shops with established reputations. It is important that the wine merchant has been in business for some years and will be for many more. Remember, it's going to be two years between the time you part with your money and the time that you receive your wine. You want to feel certain your wine merchant will not have gone into bankruptcy or taken up residence in Rio.

Remember, if ordering from out of state, you will offset the cost of shipping by not having to pay any sales tax. For instance, the sales tax of 8 percent on a $500 case of first growth Bordeaux is $40, which will be at least twice as much as UPS ground shipping from one coast to another. Points in between will be even less. Be sure to request that your wines be shipped during the fall or spring to avoid extremes of temperature during transit.

On the East Coast:

MacArthur's Liquors
4877 MacArthur Blvd., N.W.
Washingon, DC 20007
202-338-1433
www.bassins.com

Acker Merrall and Condit
160 West 72nd Street,
New York, NY 10023
212-787-1700
www.ackerwines.com

Zachy's
16 East Parkway
Scarsdale, NY 10583
1-800-723-0241
www.zachys.com

Wide World of Wines
2201 Wisconsin Avenue, NW
Washington, DC 20007
202-333-7500
www.wideworldofwines.net

In the Mid-West:

Brown Derby International Wine Center
2023 South Glenstone

Springfield, MO 65804
417-883-4066
www.brownderby.com

Sam's Wine and Spirits
1720 N. Marcey St.
Chicago, IL 60614
1-800-777-9137
www.samswine.com

On the West Coast:

K and L Wine Merchants
766 Harrison Street
San Francisco, CA 94107
1-800-437-7421
www.klwines.com
Also in Redwood City, California.

Premier Cru
5890 Christie Avenue
Emeryville, CA 94608
510-655-6691
www.premiercru.net

Bel-Air 20/20 Wine Merchants
2020 Cotner Avenue
West Los Angeles, CA 90025
310-447-2020
www.2020cotneravenue.com

Wine Club
953 Harrison Street
San Francisco, CA 94107
1-800-966-5432
Also stores in Santa Clara and Santa Ana, California.
www.thewineclub.com

Beltramo's
1540 El Camino Real
Menlo Park, CA 94025
650-325-2806
www.beltramos.com
Among some of the lowest prices in the entire country for Bordeaux
futures.

Prearrivals

Prearrivals are a sort of intermediary step between futures and actually being able to buy the wine and take it home with you. These are
wines that the retailers have purchased and will be arriving in three to
six months' time. They are usually offered at a discount, normally
about 5 percent.

Collectible Wines: The Other 90 Percent

Bordeaux, which are the most visible and have generally seen the
greatest run-up in prices as well as being the easiest to understand and
follow, are only a fraction of the world's wines that are collectible.
Numerous other wines also fit our definition of a collectible wine: *a
wine that will improve with age and will increase in price with time.*

The Wines of Burgundy

The great wines from the Burgundy region of France are not only
collectible but are arguably the greatest wines in the world. They are
also very expensive, making prices for first growth Bordeaux seem almost cheap in comparison.

The basic premise that applies to purchasing Bordeaux should also
be used in purchasing Burgundies if you are interested in seeing the
wines appreciate in value: *Buy great wines from great producers in
great years*. They are so expensive upon release, however, there is little chance that these wines will see the phenomenal appreciation that
Bordeaux from the eighties and nineties have seen.

Do your research. Again both the *Wine Advocate* and the *Wine*

Spectator do a comprehensive review of each vintage. Great years in Burgundy happen much less often than they do in Bordeaux, so when one comes along there is a feeding frenzy among consumers similar to what happens when personal injury lawyers hear of a plane crash. So beware. The problem of securing the best wines is compounded by the fact that there is very little of each, and they are highly allocated. The merchants who are able to get them almost always set them aside for their very best customers, so the average consumer's chance of buying any of the top wines is very slight.

The Great Wines and Producers of Red Burgundy

Wines

Romanee-Conti
La Tache
Grands Echezeaux
Richebourg
Chambertin
Romanee-St. Vivant
Chambertin-Clos de Bèze
Musigny
Vosne-Romanee
Clos de Vougeot
Charmes-Chambertin

Producers

Domaine de la Romanee-Conti
Domaine Leroy
Louis Jadot
Ponsot
Armand Rousseau
Jean Gros
Joseph Roty
Hubert Lignier
Meo Camuzet
Mongeard-Mugneret

Two white Burgundies that justify collecting from an investment standpoint are Montrachet and Batard Montrachet. Capable of improving and aging for twenty years or more, they are as expensive as the top red Burgundies.

Italian Wines

Certain Italian reds, like the Barolos, Barbarescos, and some of the reserve Chiantis have the ability to improve with age, though until recently the collector base for them seemed to be pretty much limited to Italy, perhaps because the top wines did not have extensive foreign distribution. This picture began to change when a new wave of Italian winemakers led by Angelo Gaja and Piero Antonori came on the scene about twenty years ago. Adopting winemaking techniques more closely resembling the techniques of the French than their Italian predecessors, they made wines that were not only more accessible but often softer and less tannic. In addition to using the traditional Nebbiolo and Sangiovese grape varieties they also planted Cabernet Sauvignon and Merlot, which they blended with the Italian varietals. Dubbed Super Tuscans by the *Wine Spectator*, the name caught on with the public while the wines received critical acclaim and consumer demand. Like Bordeaux and California Cabernet Sauvignon, these wines have seen a steady increase in demand and price. Today, the most highly sought-after wines often cost more than $200 a bottle upon release. So far, a futures market for top-end Italian wines has not been established.

For cellaring and aging, the Super Tuscans claim the most attention, wines such as Sassicaia, Ornellaia, Massetto, Solaia, and Tignanello, all with remarkable aging potential. From Piedmont, the star has always been Angelo Gaja with his blockbuster Barbaresco wines. But while every major collector has a Sassicaia or a Gaja wine in his or her cellar, not all of us can afford the expense, even if we could locate these sought-after wines. Needless to say, but we will anyway, less expensive wines in the $50 price range will also age gracefully, such as Brunello di Montalcino and vineyard-designated Chianti Classico Riserva. Look for Chianti Classico Riserva from Castello di Fonterutoli, Castello dei Rampolla, Castello d'Ama, Castello di Brolio, and Villa Cafaggio. Brunello di Montalcino producers are Casanova di Neri Tenuta Nuova, Val di Suga, and Poggio Antico.

Rich, complex Amarone from the Veneto region will age for decades. The wines take on a Port-like quality after the grapes are partially dried on straw mats before fermentation. Respected producers such as Allegrini, Masi, and Bertani have wines around $50 although many of these labor-intensive wines go for much more.

Piedmont producers of Barolo and Barbaresco, other than Angelo Gaja, honor your cellar at much smaller prices. Some of the best vineyards for Barolo are Cannubi, Cerequio, or Brunate, and for Barbaresco the vineyards of Asili and Rabaja are prized. Michele Chairlo makes Barolo from both Cannubi and Cerequio at $70, Sandrone makes a Cannubi Barolo, and Altare, Clerico, and Vietti do likewise. At half the price of a Gaja wine, Marchesi di Gresy makes three Barbarescos, Martinenga at $42, Gaiun at $60, and Camp Gross at $50. Moccagatta and Produtori del Barbaresco are other producers in the same price range.

A great guide for establishing top age-worthy Italian wines, many of which are very reasonably priced, is the Gambero Rosso list of wines that win the "three glasses" award each year. There you will find an array of producers from throughout Italy whose wines merit collecting. In addition to the guide, you can find the list on the website at www.gamberorosso.IT.

Vintage Ports

There are a variety of Ports, all of which are enjoyable, but for collecting purposes, you should stick to *vintage Ports*. Vintage Ports are only from very good to great years when a number of the port houses or producers get together and declare a year to be a vintage year. Rarely do the same producers declare two years in a row to be vintage years, nor do they always agree that a particular year should be declared. Occasionally, in a great year, every house will declare or make a vintage Port.

According to many connoisseurs, vintage Ports not only improve with age, but they insist you need to lay them down. We're not in accord with this point of view. Vintage Ports drink very well young, when their fruit is almost explosive, yet they definitely have the ability to change and gain in complexity with aging, but not without a loss of some of that wonderful, exuberant fruit.

Their ability to be consumed with great enjoyment at any stage of their evolution is an especially endearing quality of Port, for unlike Bordeaux and Cabernet Sauvignons, they do not go through what is referred to as a "dumb period" in which the wines close down or are not showing their potential. This period can last as long as a decade.

Vintage Ports have not seen the incredible appreciation of the Bordeaux first and super second growths, and even though they do invariably increase in value, at times it seems to be at a glacial pace. In fact, you can often find fifteen-year-old vintage Ports at better prices than current releases, though we suspect this in an abnormality in the market that is bound to change. If you find them, we suggest that you buy them. There is a rubber band effect in the wine market. Prices can languish for years and then suddenly catapult several hundred percent.

Recent top years are 1977, 1983, 1985, and 1994. The two top-rated Ports from Fonseca and Taylor from the 1994 vintage sell at over a $150 a bottle.

Other leading Port houses are:

Graham
Dow
Warre Noval
Cockburn
Croft

You can still find some of the Ports from 1983 and 1985 at less than $50 a bottle. If you like your Port with some bottle age, these are terrific bargains. Costing around $35 on release, they have seen little price increase. How long this will last is certainly questionable given the ever-increasing customer base for fine wines. After stocking up on Bordeaux and Cabernets, collectors will seek to broaden their collections. Wines like vintage Port and fine Sauternes are likely candidates.

Sauternes

Sauternes is a sweet dessert wine, made primarily from the semillion grape, which has been attacked by *botrytis,* also called "noble rot." The grape shrivels, and the juices become concentrated with intense flavors and a very high sugar content. The greatest of the Sauternes is Château d'Yquem. Workers are sent through the field numerous times, each time picking only those individual grapes that are just right. Extremely labor intensive, the process results in one of the world's great wines, albeit, a very expensive one, though one whose price is actually justified as much by the costs of production as by demand.

Although Château d'Yquem is in a class of its own, quite a few other Sauternes are outstanding and constitute real bargains given their quality. If you have never tasted a fine Sauternes, try one. A Sauternes is usually served after the meal and is so rich it easily substitutes for dessert. The French often serve it before a meal with Pâté de Foie Gras. The rich creamy texture of the pate is matched by the unctuous feel of the Sauternes. These wines, as they age, become the rich color of old gold.

Outstanding Sauternes producers whose wines are likely in the years to come to appreciate in value are:

d'Yquem
Suduirant
Climens
Rieussec

Other fine Sauternes such as d'Arche, Guiraud, Coutet, Nariac, and Coutet, while less likely to be in demand by collectors, are still excellent wines. Recent outstanding years for Sauternes have been 1983, 1986, 1988, and 1995. Price appreciation has been relatively small, even for d'Yquem, so these wines are usually less than double their initial release price and are an excellent bargain given their quality. These are wines to collect if you enjoy them.

German Wines

The German wines, the Trockenbeerenausleses and the Beeren-ausleses, made from the Johannisberg Riesling grapes by top producers in outstanding years are some of the world's greatest wines and command prices commensurate with their quality. In other words, they are very expensive to begin with and only become more so with age. Since the quantities of these wines are small, demand has always been greater than supply. Intensely complex and very, very sweet, these wines are what must have been meant by the expression "nectar of the gods." These wines should be sipped, drop by drop, such is their intensity. Top wines are in the $400 to $600 range. Before investing in these wines, read the reviews of Parker and the *Wine Spectator.*

The Trockenbeerenausleses and Beerenausleses are the sweetest of the German wines, capable of aging for over a hundred years, and stand at the pinnacle of the German wine pyramid. Beneath them are the Ausleses, Spätleses, and Kabinett wines, each less sweet than the one above it. You can find some great wine bargains among these wines. With a much greater supply available, prices for these great German wines are not in the stratosphere like the Trocken and Beeren-ausleses.

Another factor that has kept prices down has been the attitude of many wine drinkers that sweet wines are less sophisticated than dry wines. Another strike against them in America is that peoples' sense of what Johannisberg Riesling tastes like is based on the pleasant if banal Rieslings that are made in the United States. An apt analogy would be if we were to dismiss French Burgundies because the American wines that have been labeled Burgundy or Red Burgundy are less than awe-inspiring.

Not only are these wines of world-class stature, but they can age gracefully over twenty or more years. A bottle of J.J. Prum's 1983 Wehlener Sonnenuhr Auslese was an absolutely memorable experience. It was vibrant, with layers and layers of fruit and just the right touch of sweetness. People who are accustomed to drinking only dry wines are awed by how delicious it is and are amazed by its balance and grace.

Curiously, even as Americans' culinary tastes have expanded beyond a basic meat-and-potatoes diet to more exotic cuisines and foods, we have steadfastly continued to drink dry wines that are inappropriate as an accompaniment to spicier foods such as Thai, Cajun, Mexican, Hunan, Indonesian, and Indian. The pairing of a rich buttery Chardonnay with spicy Indian curry can be a big disappointment, whereas a German Riesling Kabinett with its slight touch of residual sugar seems to be much more suitable and satisfying. Perhaps just as Americans' taste in food has become more adventuresome, so also their willingness to try wines other than Merlot, Cabernet Sauvignon, and Chardonnay will develop.

Unfortunately, a selection of German wines is rarely available at most wine shops or in supermarkets. It's a catch 22. Merchants don't carry them because people don't buy them. People can't buy them because the wine merchants don't carry them.

Another strike against German wine acceptance is the complexity of their labels. To wine drinkers unfamiliar with all the Germanic nomenclature, trying to select a bottle of wine is an overwhelming task. So why bother? *Because German wines, given their price-to-quality ratio, are often great bargains*. Bargains don't always come easy. So what to do?

One place to start is the *Wine Advocate*, which once a year does a comprehensive review of German wines. If you don't want to subscribe, it's still possible to purchase individual back issues. The *Wine Advocate* usually gives the name and telephone number of the importer of the wines it reviews. If a wine strikes your fancy, a phone call to the importer will put you in touch with the wine merchant nearest you who carries the wine you are interested in. If he carries one or more of the wines that Robert Parker has reviewed, he's likely to have a good selection of German wines and will be able to guide you through the labyrinth of German wine. Besides the *Wine Advocate*, the *Wine Spectator* and the *Wine Enthusiast* also do thorough and comprehensive reviews of German wines, though they do not include the names and telephone numbers of the importers, so tracking down any of the wines they review is very difficult.

Three retailers on the West coast who carry a good selection of German wines are Dee Vine Wines, Premier Cru, and the Wine Club.

Both will ship to you. If you are interested in trying German wines, get on their mailing list.

As with anything that has a finite supply, if demand increases, prices will invariably rise. While we can't predict the tastes of the wine-buying public, should German wines come back into vogue, then older, well-stored examples of the better wines will gain substantially in price. If you find you enjoy them, we recommend buying and storing them properly. And maybe in ten or fifteen years you will look back and think how relatively little you paid for the gems resting in your cellar. If they don't appreciate, so what? You will be drinking terrific wines nonetheless.

Wines from the Rhône Valley

The wines from the Rhône Valley have been generating more and more interest over the last ten years. Divided into the Northern and Southern Rhône, the notable wines of Hermitage and Côte Rôtie are both expensive and collectible, though they have not seen the spectacular escalation in prices that Bordeaux and Burgundy have experienced. The Southern Rhône is famous for the wines of Châteauneuf-du-Pape. With a few exceptions the wines were not high on collectors' lists. However, outstanding vintages in 1988 and 1989 spurred interested in the wines from the area that has continued to grow as consumers discovered just how good these wines are. After ten years of okay vintages, 1998 and 1999 look like back-to-back blockbuster vintages. Prices have risen dramatically but are still almost reasonable in comparision with Bordeaux and Burgundy prices.

8

Insuring and Selling Your Wines

As your wine collection grows, its value will increase. After five years or so, you may decide to take stock, or you may look through some auction catalogs and retail price lists for older wines and realize your collection is worth thousands of dollars. Some wines have appreciated greatly, some not at all, but the fact is that your collection is valuable and subject to all the risks and perils that other household valuables are subject to, such as theft, fire, flood, earthquake, and storm damage. If the value of your wine collection is under $5,000, your homeowner or renter's insurance policy is probably adequate, though it's surprising how quickly the money for personal property covered by your insurance is used up to replace furniture, clothing, and personal property other than wine. Replacing a wine collection rarely has priority with a spouse, who always thought there were better things to spend the money on in the first place and who probably never realized how much money you were spending on it either.

So if your collection has a value of over $5,000, it is a good idea to get extra insurance to cover its replacement, especially if you live in an area of above-normal risk. The same is true for any wines stored outside your residence. Speak with your insurance agent about additional personal property insurance or contact Oldfield Brokerage Corporation.

Oldfield Brokerage Corp.
1-800-754-7124
www.wine-insure.com

Oldfield Brokerage Corporation is the administrator and broker for an insurance plan underwritten by Traveler's Insurance, the red umbrella folks, that is specifically designed to cover wine, whether a private collection or a commercial inventory. The policy provides what they call *All Risk* and includes such threats to your wine collection as earthquake, flood, landslide, volcanic action, hurricane, riots, theft, vandalism, loss of public electrical power for over twenty-four hours, and breakage in transit. There are a few exclusions to the *All Risk*, such as nuclear contamination, war, and heaven forbid, you accidentally drop that magnum of 1929 Lafite, or seizure by the government, a problem if you've been doing something illegal to augment your income, like dealing drugs. As is often the case, the more coverage you buy, the less you pay. The cost of coverage for up to $50,000 is $300, for up to $100,000 the price is $500, and $900 gets you $200,000 of insurance. Plus, there is a one time $75 membership fee. A nice feature of the policy is that there is automatic coverage of up to $25,000 for the first ninety days on newly acquired wine.

How does the insurance company determine what was actually in a collection that has been utterly demolished by a flood or earthquake? Gene Nieges of Oldfield Brokerage Corp. says that you can substantiate your claim if you have itemized sales receipts for the wines in your collection. It is a good idea to keep them in a safety deposit box. Keeping them in the house that was destroyed with your wines is definitely a bad idea.

But unless you foresaw the need to keep your reciepts when you first started your collection years ago, the odds are that you probably don't have proof for all the wines you own. In this case, you'll need an appraisal of your wine collection. Vintage Estates and Wines, Inc., which is associated with Oldfield Brokerage, can provide you with one. The telephone number is 1-800-754-7124.

There are also independent appraisers who advertise in the *Wine Spectator*. As always, do some comparison shopping to determine the best price, and check with the insurance agent to be sure that he or she will accept your choice of appraiser. If you live in a area that is at high risk from earthquakes, floods, hurricanes, and so on, and your wine collection is worth more than $20,000, insurance is something you should give some very serious consideration to.

Selling Your Wines

There may come a time when you find that you need to sell some or all of your wine collection. You can:

Sell your wines at auction.
Sell your wines directly to a retailer.
Sell your wines on commission through a retailer.
Sell your wines to friends or other collectors.
Donate your wines to charity.

Selling Your Wines at Auction

Most of the wines sold at auctions come from private collectors who for one reason or another decide to part with some or all of their wines. The wines being offered for sale are called consignments. A consignment can be a single bottle, if very rare and costly, or a large amount of wines numbering hundreds of cases. Auction houses receive consignments from estates in probate; from divorce proceedings where the court requires the couples' assets, including wine, be divided; from people with medical problems that prevent them from continuing to drink wine; even from people who convert to a religion that does not allow drinking.

However, most people who consign their wines for sale do so for more mundane reasons. They have far too much of a certain type of wine in their collection and realize they will never drink it all; their preferences in wines change; or as is commonly the case, they realize that the wines in their collection have appreciated to such an extent that they don't feel comfortable drinking them. Wines purchased for $30 a bottle that now fetch $300 a bottle will cause all but the wealthiest collectors to think twice about pulling a cork.

How do you go about selling some or all of your wines at auction? First you need to do a little homework.

1. *Contact several of the auction houses listed on page 160* and ask them to send you information about upcoming auctions as well as their guidelines and policies for selling wine.

2. *Find out the minimum consignment an auction will accept.* If, for example, you have a couple of bottles of 1975 Chateau Haut Brion that you'd like to sell, you will probably find that the auction house won't accept it since it does not fulfill their minimum dollar requirements for consignment, often $3,000 or more. If your wines don't meet the auctions' minimums, see below for other places to sell your wines.

3. *Ask for an appraisal from several auction houses.* Appraisals are calculated guesses as to what a particular lot of wines will bring at auction based on the factors of scarcity, rarity, market demand, condition of the wines, who has owned them, and who is now selling them. Auction-house appraisers consider these and numerous other factors when arriving at their estimates. For example, a case of 1961 Petrus in perfect condition, direct from the winery's cellars, will be appraised three to ten times higher than a case of 1961 Petrus with soiled and damaged labels, low fills (where the level of wine is at or below the shoulder of the bottle), or one that has passed through several hands.

The purpose of getting several appraisals is that often one market is more favorable for certain wines than others. California Cabernet Sauvignon tends to bring much better prices on the West Coast than it does on the East Coast, whereas auction prices for Bordeaux are often stronger on the East Coast than on the West Coast.

One way to get some kind of handle on what wines are doing well at what auctions is from the *Wine Spectator's* quarterly review of the high and low prices realized at a number of auctions for certain wines like 1982 Bordeaux first and second growths as well as a number of other benchmark wines. Another way is to get catalogs from previous auctions with the prices the different lots fetched.

4. *Compare what the different auction houses charge you to sell your wine.* This is what the auction houses call the seller's commission. It is the percentage of the sale price that the auction house keeps

for itself. The percentage ranges from less than 10 percent to more than 25 percent, depending on the house and the value of the wine you are selling. If you are Andrew Lloyd Webber and are getting rid of several million dollars worth of rare Bordeaux, the auction house will reduce the seller's commission significantly because of the value of the wine you are selling and also because you are famous. Famous people's collections generate a lot of interest as well as higher prices, an excellent reason not to bid at these auctions, as the prices are always inflated.

An interesting side note to Andrew Lloyd Webber's sale was that it was advertised as the collection of Andrew Lloyd Webber, with each case branded with the initials ALW. What people did not realize was that the wines never resided in his cellar because Mr. Webber never took personal possession of them. Instead they were stored in a warehouse and the cases branded with ALW so they wouldn't be confused with other wines stored there. Yet people paid a premium to own these wines because of who he is. One can imagine the conversation as the wine is poured at table, "Yes, this wine is from the collection of Andrew Llyod Webber." Do we hear a few strains of "Phantom of the Cellar"?

Few of us have collections or reputations of such grandeur, so we can expect to be charged a significant amount in seller commissions. Generally the house will charge you less the more you sell. For instance, if the wines you sell at auction go for $1,750 they may charge you 25 percent. If they sell for $5,000, they will charge you considerably less, maybe 15 percent. Find out what the percentages are. They vary from auction house to auction house, but percentage is only one part of the equation when you are determining which auction to consign your wines to.

Another factor to consider is where your wines are most likely to bring the best price. How much your wines sell for can vary dramatically from auction to auction. For example, California Cabernet Sauvignons tend to do much better at Butterfield and Butterfield, a West Coast auction firm, than they do at the East Coast auctions. Why? Bidders at the East Coast auctions are more interested and more familiar with European wines. So a 5 percent difference in seller premiums may be more than offset by much lower prices.

All the information you can marshall will help put the odds on your side, but you should realize that in the final analysis, selling your wine at auction is still a gamble. Any number of factors can come into play: a shaky stock market, at what point your lots come up for sale during the auction, a recent article in a wine magazine praising or lambasting the wines you are selling—occurrences such as these will probably have more impact than what auction house sells your wine.

It should be noted that at the present time Acker Merral and Condit do not charge the seller a commission, unlike the other auction houses.

5. *Put a reserve on the wines you are auctioning.* A reserve is the minimum amount you will accept for your wines. If no one bids the minimum, the wines remain in your possession. It's your security blanket, but it comes with a price.

If your wines don't sell, the auction house will impose a reserve fee, usually 10 percent of the reserve price. Thus if your minimum price or reserve was $4,000, expect to pay $400 in reserve fees if your wine does not sell. This fee is often waived if the seller allows the auction to set the reserve. However, if the seller wants to set a higher reserve, and the wine doesn't sell, expect to pay the fee. There is another fee, which you have to pay, whether or not your wines sell. It's the insurance fee, usually 1.5 percent of the reserve, or if the wine sells, 1.5 percent of the selling price.

It Can Be Some Time Before Anyone Shows You the Money

It usually takes from three to six months from the time you decide to sell your wines at auction until you receive a check for them. After deciding which auction you want to use to sell your wines, you then need to arrange to have the wines shipped there. Usually the auction house wants the wines in their possession at least two months before the date of the sale, so that they can be inspected, assigned lot numbers, and the descriptions put in the catalog. If you're looking for immediate cash or are hoping to catch the current market price, auctions may not be the route for you. Nor are auctions the way to go for people who have a low threshold for the unforeseen or the unexpected.

One of the few absolutes at an auction is that *there is no guarantee what price your wine will sell for.*

It Can Be Quite a Ride

Selling your wines at auction can be a roller-coaster ride. You have the possibility of seeing your wines caught up in a bidding war and the prices they ultimately bring double or even triple your expectations. You can see the broad auction market for your wines rise anywhere from 10 percent to 50 percent from the time you ship them off until the time they are sold.

On the other hand you may catch the roller coaster, not on its way up, but on its way down. One scenario could be that the market for the wines you are selling suddenly becomes soft or even goes into a tailspin. Witness the prices for 1982 Bordeaux in 1998. Another scenario could be that even though the market for your wines as a whole is strong, at a particular auction your lot may fail to instill any enthusiasm and go for a lot less than you expect it to. It's even possible that two identical lots will bring two widely different prices at the same auction. For example, two lots of 1985 Heitz Martha's Vineyard come up at auction. The first one sees an active bidding war between two collectors, pushing the price several hundred dollars above the auction average for the wine. The second lot comes up, perhaps a couple of hours later. The collector who got the first lot has gone home. Now there is only one serious bidder, who gets the second lot for hundreds of dollars less, perhaps even considerably below what the auction average has been. If your wine was the first lot, you're whistling a happy tune. If it was the second, you're probably humming something like the "Volga Boatman" or a similar funeral dirge.

For more information about auctions, see the next chapter.

Other Places to Sell Your Wine

If the uncertainties of selling your wine at auction leaves you with butterflies in your stomach or, worse still, tossing and turning during the night as you second guess yourself, then you are probably better off selling your wines through one of several other options available to you.

Selling Your Wines to Retailers

The easiest, most obvious, and often the best way to sell your wine is to *sell them to one of the large fine wine merchants.* If you have wines they want, they will generally offer you between 50 and 65 percent of the going retail rate, depending on the condition of your wines and how quickly they feel they can sell them. By the time you consider the seller's commission that the auction house charges you, the cost of insuring and shipping your wine to the auction, the several months delay before you get your money, plus the possibility that your wines may not even sell at what you expect them to, selling your wines directly to a retailer may make a lot of sense. Many of the large retailers listed in chaper 2 will purchase wines from collectors.

Another resource is to be found in the classified ad section of the *Wine Spectator* where there are numerous ads under the heading, "Business Opportunities" placed by retailers and brokers seeking to buy wines from collectors. There is nothing subtle about the bold claims of *Absolutely the Top Prices Paid, Get the Highest Price for Your Quality Collection, I Will Top Any Offer for Your Wine,* or *No One Outbids Me.*

These claims are generally from reputable merchants or brokers, who are trying to buy wines and make a substantial profit from them. Curiously, some of them will not even respond to your letter of inquiry even to say they aren't interested. Don't take it personally. They're either busy, not interested, or out of business. Those who do respond often take several weeks or months to do so. Not surprisingly, almost all will offer you much the same price, despite claims that "We always beat the competition."

If you have the time and the energy, you might want to contact four or five of the more intriguing solicitations with a list of the wines you have for sale. Depending on the wines, it is possible that one buyer will be willing to pay substantially more than the others, especially if he knows he has several clients to whom he can quickly sell the wines. As with many aspects of buying and selling wines, serendipity plays a big part.

Selling Your Wines on Commission

Another option that some of the retailers offer is to *sell your wines on commission*, usually taking around 20 percent of the price. Instead of getting 50 to 65 percent of retail for your wine, you will be getting 80 percent. You mutually agree on the figure your wine is to be priced at. The merchant will tend to want to price it lower than you do, simply because he wants to move it quickly. Usually it's a price that you can live with, plus the odds are you will see the money for the wine sooner.

If you are not in a hurry for the money this is definitely one of the easier and better ways to sell your wines. Your wine is put in the merchant's newsletter, which oftentimes reaches tens of thousands of customers. So if your wine is one that there is demand for, it will probably sell quickly if properly priced.

It's pretty much a win-win situation for both parties. The merchant gets to sell wine for which he has not made any capital outlay. You get access to the merchant's large customer base, and when your wines are sold, you realize a larger return than if you sold them directly to the wine merchant.

Sell Your Wines Privately

One other way to sell your wines is to *sell them to friends or other collectors*. Make up a list of the wines and your asking prices. Make a number of xerox copies, which you will carry with you to tastings. Inevitably, people strike up conversations during the course of these events. Often, even if the the person you're talking with is not interested, they may have friends or acquaintances who might be and can pass on your wine list to them.

Donating Your Wines to Charity

Donating your wines to charity is beneficial for everyone concerned. Admittedly, you don't get an actual cash payment for your wines, but you do get a generous tax deduction as the IRS will generally allow you to deduct top market value for your donation. Suppose you decide to donate a case of 1990 Silver Oak Napa Valley Cabernet Sauvignon to a charity auction. If you find a retailer in Beverly Hills selling the exact same wine you donated for $1,300, you can claim that as the value of your donation. Since the money raised at charity auctions is going for a good cause, it is often the case that the prices realized are often well above market value. If the case of Silver Oak that you donated brings $1,800, you are entitled to claim that amount as your charitable contribution. The other big plus is the good feeling that comes from helping a worthy cause.

9

Auctions

Wine Auctions

Wine auctions are often thought to be the realm of the serious collector, like the guy who's looking for that 1869 d'Yquem or the 1901 Petrus with the unblemished label. This is unfortunate, because wine auctions are really the source of lots and lots of good and great wines, often at bargain prices.

However, there are a few caveats that the shrewd wine buyer (that's you) should cling to before entering into this exotic realm. *First caveat: Wine auction catalogs are heady, if not down right intoxicating stuff.* Wines that you have only read or heard about seem to dance before your eyes on the pages of the catalog, like so many Salomes at the court of Herod. Suddenly you find yourself beginning to wonder if your teenage son can't wait another year for braces or if perhaps the family car might make it another twenty thousand miles. It's time to get a grip. Remember, you came looking for bargains, not chapter eleven.

Auction Catalogs

The first step is to call and request a catalog. Catalogs for upcoming auctions usually cost around $20, including shipping and handling, more if there are an especially large number of lots. Interestingly, the auction house will often send you an old catalog free of charge. Request that they send along the prices at which the various lots in the old catalog went for. If you're just curious, an old catalog will serve the same purpose as a new one by acquainting you with the auction's rules and fees and providing you with a sense of the breadth and depth of the wines offered. If you have received the list of prices realized for this auction, you will be able to see what the wines you might be interested in sold for as compared with the auction house's estimate. *It's important to remember that the prices that you are looking at do not include the buyer's premium, often 15 percent. Nor do they include such extras as sales tax, shipping, and insurance.*

If, as is often the case, you see that the lots sold way over or way under the estimates, you'll quickly understand just how volatile prices can be. Estimates are based on past sales. The folks doing the estimates know their jobs and often have been doing them for years. They have experience and knowledge. What they don't have is a crystal ball. A high price for a particular lot of wine usually indicates that several bidders were interested and thus ran the price up, but if the prices are much higher across the board, then that area of the market as a whole is hot. In many ways, wine prices at auction react like stock prices. In short they go up, and often then they go down. In 1997 the 1982 first growth Bordeaux were selling for $5,000 to $7,000 a case. A year later they were selling for $4,000 to $6,000 a case. Same wines, different demand. What cooled the market down? One important event was the financial crisis in the Far East. Wealthy Asian businessmen had begun to fill new wine cellars with collectible wines. For a few years, 1982 Bordeaux first growths were increasing at 50 percent to 100 percent a year because of frenzied demand. When demand dropped, so did prices. Today, these wines are back up to 1997 prices.

There is another advantage to seeing the prices paid for wines at auction. You can compare them with the price lists of the large wine merchants around the country. Often the wine that went for $300 at auction can be purchased for $175 from a retailer. Go figure. Of course, the converse is equally true. A wine may go for $175 at auction and be listed at $325 on a retailer's price list. This is one of the attractions of auctions. Scoring a great wine at a great price. Attending the auctions can be fun, especially if you like the thrill of the stock market combined with the fast-paced action of Las Vegas.

Some auction houses make the wines available for inspection prior to the sale, others don't. Some offer presale tastings (for a fee). Let the catalog be your guide. It will describe how and where the wines have been stored, such as "Removed from Temperature-Controlled Storage." This tells the buyer that the wines have been stored at a consistent temperature, usually around 55 degrees Fahrenheit and so will not have been subjected to extremes of hot or cold. Or a number of different small lots might be headed "Property of Various Collectors." Normally, each lot has been in the possession of one collector until it arrives for sale at auction. If the wine in the lot has been owned by several collectors, it is possible that the wine has been stored under a variety of conditions. However, if this posed a serious problem to the wines, wine auctions would not be in business for long. The odds are pretty good that almost all of the wine has been lovingly taken care of from the time of purchase by the original owner. If the auction houses see any obvious signs of poor storage, they will reject the consignment, but then again, *nothing is guaranteed.* For instance, if the wine is corked, it's yours. You can't return it like you can at a restaurant or to a wine merchant.

The catalogs also describe the wines themselves in detail. Lot 2019 of eight bottles of 1982 Château Latour might have this description:

Pauillac, Premier Cru Classe
Glue stained labels, slightly oxidized capsules
1 vts, 1 with slight evidence of weepage
Estimate 2,750/3,250

Let's define what is meant by some of the terms used in the auction catalog's description. Capsules are the foil coverings over the necks of the bottles. Vts stands for very top shoulder. The shoulder is the curved part of the bottle between the neck and the straight sides. Vts would indicate that the level of the wine in the bottle is probably ½ inch below the neck. Weepage refers to the fact that some of the wine has escaped from the bottle and run down below the foil where it has dried. It suggests that the bottle of wine may have a faulty cork or been exposed to high heat at one time.

The fact that not all the labels are perfect, the capsules are slightly oxidized, some of the wine has evaporated from one of the bottled (vts) and another shows signs of weepage, will all affect the estimate as well as the sale price, perhaps by as much as 15 to 30 percent, compared with eight bottles in pristine condition. Many collectors buy only wines in bottles that are in perfect condition, so are willing to pay a premium. This is also true of restaurants that do not want to present an expensive bottle of wine in less than perfect condition to a customer.

Bruce Kaiser at Butterfield and Butterfield Auctions points out that labels of wines stored under the proper humidity for a number of years will become wrinkled or stained from mold growing on them. In fact, the Châteaux in Bordeaux do not label their bottles from older vintages until they are ready to release them.

So if you are primarily interested in drinking the wine, wines with torn or damaged labels and oxidized capsules can often be purchased at great prices, relative to what one would pay for the same wine in perfect bottles. If a torn label is an embarrassment, the wine can be poured into a crystal decanter and brought to the dinner table. The wine will taste the same as wine from a pristine bottle, only it will have cost you considerably less.

Bidding At Auction

If you have never purchased wine at auction, the people who work for the auction houses suggest that you study the catalog carefully and then attend an auction without bidding. This experience will give you a feel for the atmosphere, which is very fast paced and a little confusing at first. At Butterfield and Butterfield wine auctions, 230 to 250 lots an hour will be knocked down by the auctioneer. That's one approximately every 15 seconds. Bids are coming not only from the floor, but by special telephone hookups in other parts of the country, and from absentee bidders, who are represented by the auction house. You can easily get caught up in auction fever by the fast pace and with the enormous amounts of money spent in a matter of seconds. This is why it's good to have a practice run. See how you react to this atmosphere. It's not the same as playing with Monopoly money.

Another piece of advice that experienced bidders always offer: *Set a limit on how much you want to spend for each lot and for the day and stick to it.* This is probably easier said than done.

Say there are eight lots of wine that interest you, ranging in price from $300 to $1,200, with a total estimated value of $4,500/$5,800. Go through the list, set the price you want to pay for each one. Then figure the maximum you are willing to spend for the whole day, let's say $1,500. It's apparent you cannot buy all the wines you are interested in, so rank your choices from first to last. What lot is the one you really want most? This is the one to be careful about, and this is the one that will cause you to throw reason and money out the window if you get caught up in a bidding war.

The main advantage of attending the auction in person is that you can manage your bidding better. If you get a good deal on an early lot, you can spend a little more on the next lot on your wish list. Another reason to come to the auction is that if you really want a certain lot, you don't want to lose it by one bid.

However, the converse is also true. It's easy to get caught up in a bidding war and spend far more than you intended.

Multiple Lots of the Same Wine

Oftentimes there will be multiple lots of the same wine. Let's say there are eleven single-case lots of 1979 Jordan Alexander Valley Cabernet Sauvignon. It's a wine you would like to have in your collection. Estimate is $275/$375.

This is a situation where the games begin. The chances of getting a case at a bargain price is good, because there are so many cases available. Generally, the highest prices are realized on the first couple of lots, because this is when the folks who really want the wine are bidding to secure it. Then interest begins to wane a bit and the case price drops 20 percent. You think to yourself, "This is the time to bid." But in the back of your mind, you're thinking, "If it's come down this far, it will probably come down even more if I just wait." So you wait. And the price continues to drop on the next couple of cases. At this price the wine is a steal, so you decide to bid on the next lot. However, other folks interested in the wine feel the same way. The price goes up. There are only five cases left, and each lot goes for more than the last, until it's almost back to the price the first couple of lots brought.

Moral: There is no foolproof way to know when the price has hit bottom.

Another scenario that gets played out with multiple lots of the same wine is that sometimes the auction house announces before bidding starts that the winning bidder on the first lot has *the option to buy as many of the remaining lots as he wants for the same price.* Sometimes the price is a steal because other bidders have held back, guessing that the price will come down as more and more of the lots are sold. If the winning bidder is a retail store or a restaurant, it may very well exercise its option to buy the remaining lots of the 1979 Jordan, leaving the rest of the interested bidders moaning and hitting themselves in the head with their paddles.

Mixed Lots

A mixed lot is a number of different wines, generally with some kind of theme. It can be as specific as a lot of various California Cabernet Sauvignons from the late 1970s or as general as something titled "Red Wine Collection." It can be a couple of bottles, or it can be several cases of wine. Some have been put together by experienced collectors and sometimes the auction house puts them together. Often they contain highly sought-after wines along with some that are not so popular. The good mixed lots afford the buyer an opportunity to obtain, often at very reasonable prices, a group of wines that reflect the intelligence and diligence of an avid collector.

Here's such an example of a mixed lot from a recent auction. The lot contains eleven bottles of Port.

Dow's 1970	(2 bottles)
Martinez 1970	(2 bottles)
Warre's 1970	(1 bottle)
Warre's 1977	
1 soiled label	(2 bottles)
Fonseca 1977	(1 bottle)
Graham's 1977,	
Stained label	(1 bottle)
Ramos-Pinto 1983	(1 bottle)

Quinto do Vesuvio 1990
Cracked wax capsule   (1 bottle)
Estimate 500/600

The actual price realized was $690. If whoever purchased this lot was new to vintage Ports, that person has also bought a wine education.

Mixed lots can offer more than just the wines in them. They offer a unique opportunity to compare and to learn about wines that might no longer be available. They provide the buyer with a chance to try wines he may never have heard of or might not normally buy. Sometimes, these wines are the real gems of the lot.

Absentee Bidding

Most wine bought at auction is purchased, not by the folks in the auction room, but by absentee bidders. Absentee bidding allows people from across the country and around the world to bid on wines without having to be in the room. They have asked the auction house to bid for them, according to guidelines and price limits that the absentee bidder has established beforehand.

There are a number of advantages to absentee bidding, first of which is that a person in Fairbanks, Alaska, doesn't have to fly to New York to bid on that lot of 1990 Pinot Noir that he wants. Big savings on airfare! Another advantage is that the absentee bidder can't get caught up in auction fever and spend twice as much as he had planned, because he tells the auction house the maximum he will spend for a given lot. The auction house bids for him until that amount is reached and then drops out. The absentee bidder's emotions are kept out of the bidding process.

How Does Absentee Bidding Work?

1. Get a catalog for the next auction.
2. Look through it and find those lots that interest you.

If you have a couple of previous catalogs with the lists of prices in them, you'll have an idea if the estimates are low or high. Check the prices versus the prices in the catalogs from some of the larger wine merchants. *In short: Do your research.*

3. Determine how much you are willing to spend for each lot. Be sure to factor in the auction commission, usually 15 percent (it is distinct from, and should not be confused with the seller's commission) and applicable sales tax if you live in the state where the auction is held.

4. Determine how much you want to spend in total.

5. Fill out the absentee bidder forms in the catalog.

You are establishing your credit and selecting the lots and amount you are willing to spend on each.

6. Put in writing the total amount you wish to spend, so the auctioneer will stop bidding when that amount is reached. Include any special instructions. Call to verify that they understand the instructions.

7. Now sit back and wait. On the day of the auction, the absentee clerk will try to bid just as you would, in order to obtain the item at the lowest price possible. The clerk will be bidding against people in the audience as well as other absentee bidders and will continue to bid for you until she is successful or until she reaches your bid limit and has to drop out.

8. To find out the hammer price, you can call an automated auction results line following the auction. One note of caution. Just because the hammer price was the same as the top amount you were willing to spend for a lot, doesn't necessarily mean the wine is yours. There may have been several bids at that price. In cases of a tie, the lot goes to the absentee bidder who sent in his paperwork first.

9. If successful, you'll receive an invoice within a few days.

Some More Information About Wine Auctions

Don't hesitate to call the auction house's customer service department with any question, no matter how dumb it may seem to you. They want to make the auction process as intelligible and enjoyable as possible.

Most lots have a minimum price, or reserve, that is somewhere below the low estimate. The auctioneer generally starts the bidding above the minimum. Let's say on Lot 2304 the auctioneer starts the bidding at $750. You have put a bid in for $600, the reserve price. If there are no other bids, you will get the lot for the reserve price of $600, even though the bidding was started at $750.

Some people will bid, either in person or by absentee bid, well below estimate on dozens and dozens of different lots on the odd chance they'll pick up some real bargains. Sometimes they do. There are all sorts of ways to plan your approach.

Who Stands to Benefit Most from Auctions?

Bruce Kaiser at Butterfield and Butterfield feels that the folks who do best at auctions are people who like older wines and who:

1. Know what they like.
2. Have done their homework.
3. Know the prices of the wines they are interested in.
4. Know what they want to bid.
5. Know what they are willing to pay.
6. Are willing to take an occasional gamble.

Kaiser said that when he started working in the wine auction business, he quickly discovered that when you take into account the cost of wine, time, funds, storage, plus the effort it takes to build a collection, *old wines are cheaper than new wines.* This is not to dismiss the many wines that appreciate faster than a savings account. However, when you come to auction, you'll have the opportunity to purchase thousands of older wines you didn't have to store, and that you won't have to wait another ten or fifteen years for them to mature.

He also points out that auctions are especially handy for people who don't have storage for more than several cases of wine. He knows of quite a few wine buffs who live in apartments and purchase three or four lots of wine at a time, drink them, and then come back to the auction for more.

Some of the Bigger Auction Houses:

Phillips Auctioneers
New York
1-800-825-2781
Appraisal: 212-691-7744
Consignments of $5,000 and up.

Zachy's-Christie's
New York
914-723-6560

Butterfield and Butterfield
San Francisco
Catalog 1-800-223-2854 ext 525
Appraisal: 415-861-7500 ext. 363
www.butterfield.com

Acker Merral and Condit
New Jersey
201-339-9750
Note: no seller's commission.

Sotheby's with Sherry-Lehmann
New York
212-606-7050

Sotheby's
Chicago
312-396-9513

winebid.com
www.winebid.com
Online auction of fine wines.

10

Restaurants

Bringing Your Own Wine

Among the many advantages and pleasures that collecting wines provide, you will discover that being able to bring a bottle of fine wine that you purchased several years before to a restaurant to enjoy with your meal is certainly one of the most rewarding. First, you have the advantage of knowing how the wine has been stored. An older bottle of wine on a restaurant's list may have been purchased at auction, from a collector, or from another restaurant, and so may have passed through a number of hands before ending up at this particular restaurant. It's possible that the storage conditions may not always have been optimum. Second, restaurants mark their wines up anywhere from 50 to 500 percent of the current retail price. A bottle of 1982 Pichon Lalande that you purchased for less than $30 fifteen years ago may be on the restaurant's wine list at $750. Inflation like this will cause a pleasant tingle to run down your spine, knowing that you're drinking a wine that, if you hadn't brought it with you, would have required taking out a second mortgage on your house before coming to the restaurant. Though not all restaurants will allow their customers to bring their own wine, most will. It's a good idea to ask what a restaurant's policy is about bringing your own wine.

There is a certain protocol to observe when bringing wine to a restaurant. The wine you bring should not be a wine and vintage that the restaurant has on its wine list, though in the case of rare or expensive wines, this part of the protocol is often overlooked, for instance, a first growth Bordeaux or *premier cru* Burgundy.

With the exception of the most expensive restaurants, you are not likely to find many top-rated wines from highly touted vintages on their wine list. It's simply a matter of economics. Restaurants generally buy wines from recent vintages that have not received high scores in the wine press because such wines are less expensive, generally ready to drink sooner, and are more readily available. An example would be 1997 third and fourth growth Bordeaux, or midrange California Cabernets or Merlots. So if you bring in a $15 bottle of wine you just picked up at your local jug shop, and it's on the restaurant's wine list, they may get a little huffy when you ask them to pour it. In fact, they may get a little huffy even if they don't have it on their list.

Corkage fees are generally in the $10 to $15 dollar range, per bottle, though it can be higher. It is always wise to call beforehand to find out the corkage policy and charge. Also, it is always a good idea to add something extra to the tip. It's gracious, and it's fair. As a result you'll find the folks at the restaurant will be more than delighted to see you and your bottle of wine the next time.

Returning Wines

Another advantage of bringing your own wine with you to a restaurant is that you avoid a situation that occasionally can be more than a little stressful: refusing a faulty bottle of wine. The scenario generally plays out like this. The customer orders a bottle of wine, let's say a 1986 second growth from Bordeaux to accompany the meal. The waiter or sommelier nods and says "very good." He returns with the unopened wine and shows you the bottle so you can verify that this is the wine and vintage you want. You can also look at the bottle to see if any evaporation has occurred and to check for any telltale signs of poor storage. For a wine less than twenty years old, the fill should be above the shoulder and in the neck of the bottle. If it's not, ask for another bottle. Look to see if there has been any leakage, or wine stains on the cap or label. If so, the wine may have been subjected to high temperatures. Choose another wine. However, if the label has been discolored or spoiled by mold, don't worry. It just means the wine has been stored in damp conditions, which is bad for the label, but good for the wine.

If the wine is what you ordered, its fill is appropriate for its age, and there are no signs of leakage, the waiter will open the wine and show you the cork. There are several reasons for this, none of which have to do with wine snobbery. With expensive wines the winery's name will always be on the cork. Seeing the name on the cork is another assurance that you're getting the wine you're paying for. If the cork is saturated with wine, it suggests that the wine may have been subjected to very high temperatures at some time in its history. Approach such a wine with caution or ask to speak to the sommelier and express your concerns.

Okay, so you've looked at the cork and it seems up to snuff. The next step is to taste the wine. The waiter pours a small amount in your glass. You swirl the wine around while your dining companions wait for your reaction. Instead of luscious fruit aromas, the wine smells of damp cardboard, or perhaps even worse, like a cattle feed lot. The wine is corked or possibly affected by *Brettanomyces* (a strain of yeast, also known as "Brett").

This wine is flawed, and you should refuse it. The smell caused by being corked or having *Brettanomyces* ranges from subtle to disgusting and is more noticeable to some people than to others. Some wine enthusiasts feel a small amount of *Brettanomyces* adds complexity to a wine, because they appreciate the damp earth smell found in some Pinot Noirs and Burgundies.

Since you and your guests are consuming the wine, you must make the judgment whether the wine is acceptable or not. It is not the waiter's call. If the wine is flawed, send it back. Explain that you think it is faulty. Generally the maitre d' or sommelier will get in the act.

If it's an expensive bottle of wine, a maitre d' will be less likely to agree with you and may say, "I don't detect anything wrong with this wine." Simply state, as calmly as you can, that you do detect something wrong with the wine and would like it replaced. Eventually a maitre d' will acquiesce, though not without a lot of gestures, head shaking, and raised eyebrows between himself and your waiter. Expect it. Then weather it with grace and equanimity.

However, if the bottle of wine you ordered, after having read that it received a score of 100 in several wine publications, is not what you expected but seems particularly tannic and without the glorious fruit the critics had raved about, you've gotten a wine that has shut down or gone into a dumb stage (i.e., not showing its potential). Many Cabernet Sauvignon–based wines do this. Spending a lot of money for a wine that doesn't deliver is disappointing, but the restaurant is not at fault, and it will not allow you to return the wine. The best you can do in this case is ask the waiter to decant the wine and hope it will open up over the course of the evening. Or you can ask the waiter to recork the wine, so you can take it home. Be sure to put the bottle in the trunk of your car, since it is illegal to transport an open bottle of spirits in the passenger compartment of a vehicle. At home, open the wine and allow it to breathe. Try it the next night. You might be pleasantly surprised.

Can Bargains Be Found in Restaurants?

The ideal way to enjoy a good wine in a restaurant is to bring your own. You know how it's been stored, and you're not paying the markup of several hundred percent that restaurants normally charge. Sometimes it is not always possible to bring your wine. For instance, you may be on a business trip in another city and need to take clients to dinner, or you're with a group of friends after a hike or a baseball game and decide to go to a new restaurant that is reported to be really good. There's no time to run home and grab a few bottles from your cellar. What can be done to ensure that you get a good wine at a reasonable price? Here are a couple of suggestions that will stand you in good stead.

Compliment the Wine Buyer

If a restaurant prides itself on its food, it will almost always have a good wine list. If the list runs for several pages or longer, it's more than likely that someone has put a lot of time and thought into putting it together, often the sommelier or perhaps the manager. Ask to speak to that person. When he arrives, compliment him on the list, its depth, diversity, and selection. Almost everyone appreciates a job-well-done pat on the back. Next ask the wine buyer for suggestions as to which wines are the best values. He may guide you to several, perhaps some of which you may not have tasted or even heard of. Ask him which of the wines would be best suited for the entrees you are considering ordering. The odds are that the wine and food pairing will be right on—he knows the food and knows the wine, you have complimented him and asked his advice; he is not likely to let you down now. If you do not want to follow his suggestions, which may tend toward wines you are unfamiliar with, then you can ask him which Chardonnay, Merlot, or Cabernet Sauvignon he would recommend.

Choose Wines From the Region Where the Food Originated

If the restaurant has a particular geographical focus such as California cuisine, bistro fare from Provence, or the foods of Northern Italy, the wine list will be weighted with wines from the region that will complement the food. Though the wines may be unfamiliar to you, they are probably well known to the chef, and they are certain to be wines that are not only more enjoyable with the food, but will do considerably less damage to your pocketbook than a more recognizable Cabernet from Napa or Bordeaux. Ask the waiter what the chef would recommend with the dish you are ordering. Sometimes it requires a leap of faith to put your self in someone else's hands when it comes to ordering a wine, but often this is when you make great wine discoveries.

Match the Price of the Wine to That of Your Entree

If the price of the entree is over $20 choose from the less expensive wines, if under $20 choose from the more expensive wines. High-end restaurants expect most of their sales to come from the more expensive wines on their list, yet the wine buyer does not want the cheaper wines to reflect poorly on the quality of the restaurant so will go to great lengths to secure outstanding wines for the lower end of the price scale. Conversely, inexpensive restaurants know they cannot mark their high-end wines up two to three times over retail and expect to sell them, so often the upper-end wines are selling at close to retail prices, especially for older vintages, which the restaurant may have purchased upon release and have not marked up even as the prices have climbed in the retail market.

House Reds and Whites: If You're Not Sure, Ask for a Complimentary Taste

Often the house wine is *plonk*, an undistinguished jug wine from some giant producer with little or no varietal character. If the wine they are pouring is unfamiliar to you, but you feel $6 is a bit much to discover you don't like it, ask if it would be possible to have a complimentary taste. Odds are that they'll give it to you, since they want your experience to be a pleasant one.

Occasionally, depending on the restaurant and its attitude toward profit and customer relations, it can be a great bargain as well as a wonderful wine. Several years ago, Jeremiah Tower of Stars restaurant fame in San Francisco, opened a Stars cafe right next door to his famous restaurant. The food was simple and unpretentious, yet absolutely terrific and at a quarter of the price of its famous big brother. For several months they poured the current vintage of Quivara Zinfandel at $2.50 a glass as the house wine, a price even less than what one could buy it for in a store. Needless to say, we found any number of excuses to eat at Stars cafe during this time.

11

I Know Where It's From, but What's in the Bottle?

Not only are there literally thousands of different wine varietals, produced by thousands of wineries, but also several of the largest wine-producing countries, including France, Italy, and Spain, usually don't tell us what's in the bottle. If they do, it's something cryptic, like "Table Wine," "Red Table Wine," or "Still Table Wine." They are not purposefully attempting to keep us in the dark. Rather, it's more a case of, "We've been doing it this way for three hundred years. Why should we change?"

Perhaps as these countries seek a larger and larger world market, we will see the grape varietals listed somewhere on the bottle. Until that day, the consumer is left in the dark. We know it's red. We know it's from a given region, and perhaps we know how much alcohol is in it, but as far as information on the bottle as to what grapes were used to make the wine, well, we don't have the foggiest. In an effort to shine a little light on this subject, we're going to talk about these wines and the grape varietals that go into them, because often the very best expression of Cabernet Sauvignon, Merlot, Chardonnay, Pinot Noir, Syrah, Grenache, and others, come from these countries.

The Wines of France

apes used in this region of France are Cabernet Sauvignon and Merlot, though a small amount of another three varieties sometimes finds its way into the wines. Most of the knowledgeable folks in the wine world maintain the highest expression of these two grape varieties come from Bordeaux. The great wines from Pauillac such as Château Latour are almost exclusively Cabernet Sauvignon. The wines from Pomerol, such as Château Petrus are likely to be almost wholly Merlot. Most of the rest are varying percentages of the two, some having more Cab, some more Merlot.

These are the wines the rest of the world's Cabernet Sauvignons and Merlots strive to emulate. Over the past twenty years, several blind tastings, matching great vintages of California Cabernets against great vintages of first growth Bordeaux, have shown that the best wines from California can hold their own and often outdistance their French role models. Not so with Merlot. Here the French maintain uncontested superiority, as well as outrageous prices for their best.

Burgundy

The red wines from Burgundy are wholly Pinot Noir, with the *grand crus* ranking as the best in the world. Even second and third tier Burgundies have few challengers from outside the region. The problem with Burgundies is twofold. They are very expensive, and a lot of them are disappointing. But when you find a great Pinot Noir, it is a memorable experience. If you're looking for affordable Burgundies, look for the village wines from Mercurey, Ruilly, and Givry.

The white wines of Burgundy are made exclusively from the Chardonnay grape. Many feel that there isn't a Chardonnay from anywhere else in the world that can compare with the best from here. Grown on parcels of land no more than an acre or two in size, the wines are a wonderful reflection of where the grapes were raised, what the French call *terroir*. Once again, the best has its price. As much as $500 for a single bottle.

Good value white Burgundies can be found among the wines from

Macon and Chablis. Made from 100 percent Chardonnay grapes, most of the wines aren't likely to spend any time in oak, though the wines of Pouilly-Fuisse do. It ought to be noted that when the prices for white Burgundies from France and the Chardonnays from Australia and California are similar, often the quality of the wines is too.

Beaujolais

In the Beaujolais region of France, the red grape varietal is Gamay. Fruity, with high acids and low tannins, the wines pair well with a wide variety of foods and are enjoyable upon release, though the better ones will age for ten years or more. The best and most expensive wines are from ten individually designated villages with *cru* status. The "King of Beaujolais" is Georges Du Boeuf whose wines represent consistent and outstanding value. It is possible to find a large selection of his wines at between $7 and $10 a bottle.

Rhône

The Rhône region in France is divided into two parts, the northern, where Syrah is the red grape varietal responsible for the fine wines of Hermitage, Crozes-Hermitage, St. Joseph, Cornas, and Côte Rôtie. Again, only a few Syrahs made elsewhere in the world can compare with the best from here, though once past the top wines, the playing field levels out and the wines of California and Australia begin to hold their own. The wines of Crozes-Hermitage and St. Joseph offer the best values. The white wines are made from Marsanne, Viognier, and Roussanne grapes. These varietals are just now beginning to be produced in the United States with some success.

In the Southern Rhône, the most famous wines are from the appellation Châteauneuf-du-Pape. Here the laws allow the wines to be made from as many as a combination of thirteen different varietals, though most are made from a blend of between four and seven, the primary grapes being Grenache, Mourvedre, Carignan, and Syrah. The 1998 and 1999 vintages were outstanding, the best vintage since the vintages of 1989 and 1990. The prices for these wines have begun to rise, though not as fantastically as many of their more famous counterparts in France, so you have an opportunity to buy great wines at reasonable prices.

Alsace

In Alsace, unlike other regions of France, the grape varietal is listed on the bottle, perhaps because it had been part of Germany for so many years, and the Germans aren't ones for ambiguity. More than 90 percent of the wines are white: Riesling, Gewürztraminer, Pinot Blanc, and Pinot Gris are the main varietals. Except for the dessert wines, all are dry. If you've never tried a dry Riesling or dry Gewürztraminer from a good producer, you are in for a very pleasant discovery. These wines often constitute exceptional value and offer a welcome respite from Chardonnay. Importer Kermit Lynch, in an effort to acquaint his clientele with the wonderful variety of Alsatian wines, will occasionally put together a case sampler of twelve different Alsatian wines and discount the price by as much as 40 percent of the bottle price. It is quite a bargain.

Loire

The Loire Valley stretches halfway across France, as the Loire River runs from east to the west into the Atlantic Ocean. In the easternmost section, very fine wines are made from the Sauvignon Blanc grape. The two main wines are Sancerre and Pouilly-Fume, with the latter a little more full-bodied and with more pronounced mineral flavors. Selling for between $10 to $20 they are good values.

Halfway to the Atlantic, near the city of Tours, the grape is Chenin Blanc. The wines are named after the local village of Vouvray. They can be dry, slightly sweet, or sweet. The wines bear little resemblance to the many insipid Chenin Blancs grown elsewhere in the world. They range in price from $6 to $20.

In the area where the Loire empties into the Atlantic, the grape varietal is Muscadet, and that's what the wine is called. Dry, light, and great with shellfish, it's inexpensive, and is best drunk within a year or two of vintage.

Champagne

French Champagne is made from three grape varietals: Chardonnay, Pinot Noir, and Meunier, the last two are red grapes. Though the grapes are red, their juice is not, so any color is a result of leaving the skins in contact with the juice. Champagne can be made entirely from one grape or a blend of them. Most Champagne is nonvintage and is usually made from blending two years together. Each of the various Champagne houses has a certain style that it attempts to duplicate year after year. Blending vintages greatly facilitates the effort to maintain consistency. Veuve Clicquot Gold Label is one such nonvintage Champagne. Usual retail is up to $40, though it can often be found for $27, or even less. Creamy and rich in style, it's a delicious introduction to what really good Champagne is all about.

Sauternes

Perhaps the most famous sweet wines in the world, Sauternes are made from Sémillion and some Sauvignon Blanc that have been infected with *botrytis cinerea* or what the French call "noble rot," a mold that causes the grapes to shrivel, concentrating the sugars and resulting in a wonderfully rich, sweet wine. Since the world's palate is more inclined to dry wines, the prices for these beauties from Bordeaux have not seen the escalation that their red counterparts have. They are wonderful wines at affordable prices; many of the best still cost under $40 a bottle.

Wines of Italy

Piedmont

In Piedmont, the names of wines are often derived from the name of a village in the area. Wines labeled Barbaresco are from a small region in northwestern Piedmont where the village of Barbaresco is located. Here the Nebbiolo grape is responsible for some of Italy's finest wines. With abundant fruit and hard tannins, these wines have traditionally required extensive aging. Modern vinification techniques are making the tannins softer, allowing the wines to be drunk sooner. They are rich, full-bodied wines with flavors of truffles, berries, and chocolate.

The Nebbiolo grape is also used in what is often considered Italy's greatest wine, Barolo, what the Italians call, "the king of wines and the wine of kings." Made in a small area of southwestern Piedmont around the village of Barolo, the wine traditionally was extremely tannic when young and required long aging before evolving into a rich full-bodied wine. Again, changes in wine-making techniques have succeeded in moderating the harshness of the tannins, so that the wines can now be enjoyed sooner, though the Italians feel at least ten years is required. If you don't mind your wines a little on the tannic side, many can be drunk within a year of release. Be prepared to pay. Top producers like Aldo Conterno, Angelo Gaja, or Bruno Giacosa get $100 a bottle, although you can find Barolo from other producers for less, for instance Stefano Farina for about $30.

Barolo is considered the bigger and more age-worthy of the two wines made from Nebbiolo, while Barbaresco is thought to be a more elegant and refined expression of the grape. There is mixed opinion among Italians as to whether the modern techniques employed in making the wines are all beneficial. As is often the case, when something is gained, it is often at the expense of something lost. The 1995, 1996, and 1997 vintages were all exceptional.

Wines labeled Barbera are actually made from the grape varietal, Barbera. Long considered the poor stepsister of the more prestigious Nebbiolo, Barbera has recently been treated with more respect and attention by Italian winemakers with stunning results. The wines are rich, flavorful, and multidimensional. Ready to drink sooner than the Barolos and Barbarescos, they are significantly less costly and offer some of northern Italy's best red wine values. Michele Chiarlo is one of the formost producers of Barbera and has led the movement to make the massive reds of Piedmont more accessible and attractive when young.

Although less commonly found than Barbera, Dolcetto is another smooth, supple wine from the region that can be enjoyed when young and, like Barbera, is much less costly than the Nebbiolo wines.

Piedmont also produces good white wines. The first is Asti Spumante from the Moscato grape. Look for the hand-crafted version of Moscato, called Moscato d'Asti, because the former is a mass-produced bulk wine. In volume, this sparkling dessert wine is second only to Champagne, which beats it by a little. Among still whites, Gavi from the Cortese grape has emerged as one of Italy's most coveted white wines, and Arneis is attracting increasing attention.

Tuscany

In Tuscany, the primary grape varietal is Sangiovese. Tuscany rivals Piedmont in the fame of its wines and its cuisine. The most famous wine from Tuscany and also the largest appellation in the region is Chianti. The wines are made primarily from the Sangiovese grape, though numerous other varietals can be added to the blend.

In the early 1960s, the *Denominazione di Origine Controllata e Garantitia,* or DOCG as it is commonly written on labels, was established to identify the finest wines and ensure that they are made according to stringent guidelines. For instance, there are rules that declare that Chianti Classico wines can only be produced in a defined area between Florence and Siena. In the last twenty years, quality has been on an upswing because DOCG regulations have reduced yields per acre by one-third, raised the extract levels required, and radically reduced the percentage of white wine allowed into the blend. These changes, in combination with new agricultural and vinification techniques, plus investment in better equipment, have resulted in wines with more complexity, brighter fruit, and greater focus than the wines of the past.

In top years, such as 1995, 1996, 1997, 1998, and 1999, most big producers make a Chianti Normale or an I.G.T. Sangiovese, a Chianti Classico Normale or Riserva, and one or more single vineyard Riserva wines. Small producers will make wines in fewer of these categories. Prices range from $9 to $16 for Chianti Classico Normale. Riservas, which have been aged for three years before release and are considered to be of superior quality, range from $14 to $30 a bottle, and Single Vineyard Riservas go from $20 to $40 a bottle.

It is not uncommon to find excellent Normale Chiantis for around $10 a bottle. These wines offer good value as well as being in wide cir-

culation and easily available in the United States. Outstanding producers are Fontodi, Castello dei Rampolla, Villa Cafaggio, Le Corti,
Isole e Olena, and Castello della Paneretta.

Though Chianti is the best known wine from Tuscany, the wines
from hillside vineyards around the village of Montalcino, called Brunello di Montalcino, are considered some of Italy's very finest. Made
entirely from Brunello grapes, a clone of Sangiovese Grosso, the
wines are big, full-bodied, and capable of aging for decades. Biondi
Santi and Frescobaldi are well respected producers whose Brunello di
Montalcino is imported into the United States, although many other
small estates also produce the wine. Rosso di Montalcino is a younger,
less costly version made from Brunello vines.

Like Chianti, Vino Nobile di Montepulciano is a blend also made
primarily from Sangiovese with the addition of Canaiolo, Mammolo,
and other varieties in varying amounts and comes from the Montepulciano area, southeast of the city of Siena. Rosso di Montepulciano
is the younger, less costly alternative.

The Italian government's DOGC rules for each of these great
wines prescribe what grape combinations can be used and exclude all
others. Italian winemakers, chaffing under restrictions that prevented
them from adding Cabernet Sauvignon or Merlot to their wines, decided to break away from the regulations by the simple expedient of
simply calling their wines Vino da Tavola, or table wines. Today, the
new classification for Vino da Tavola is I.G.T., or Indicazione Geo-
grafica Tipica. Led by producer Piero Antinori's Solaia and Tignanello,
both different blends of Cabernet Sauvignon and Sangiovese, these
wines burst on the wine scene twenty years ago to wide acclaim. In a
stroke of fortuitous fate, the wines were dubbed "Super Tuscans" by
the *Wine Spectator.* Catchy and easy to remember, the name imbued
the new wines with immediate international cachet.

Most Super Tuscans are a blend of Sangiovese and either Cabernet
Sauvignon, Cabernet Franc, or Merlot. As demand for the wines has
increased, so have the prices. The top wines command over $200 a
bottle, though there are numerous wines in this category that fall in
the $30 to $40 range.

One of Tuscany's few white wines is the fruity Vernaccia di san
Gimignano from the ancient Vernaccia grape. In the last few years

Chardonnay, Pinot Bianco, and Pinot Grigio are developing an increasing presence, as well as the blend Galestro, which is a combination of white grapes, mainly Trebbiano, which is found throughout Italy by various names, including Greco in the south, and can make very pleasant, zesty wines.

Veneto

Veneto is the wine-growing region surrounding the city of Verona. The four most prominent wines from the area are Bardolino, Valpolicella, Amarone, and Soave.

The red wine Valpolicella is extremely popular with Italians who find it an ideal accompaniment to food. Made primarily from Corvina, Rondinella, and Molinara grapes, the wines are medium in body, fragrant, and very fruity. Some of these wines fill much the same role as Beaujolais does in France. They offer good value for a pleasant everyday drinking wine, and like Beaujolais, they are not difficult to find in the United States.

Many producers are now making richer styles of Valpolicella, using the "ripasso" method, which literally means to repass the wine over the lees of Amarone. The lees are the sediment of yeast cells and grape solids that accumulate during fermentation, so repassing Valpolicella through the Amarone lees creates a much more intense wine. Often these "repasso" wines have a proprietary name like Allegrini's Palazzo della Torre or Masi's Campo Fiorin.

Unlike Sangiovese, and to a lesser extent Barbera and Nebbiolo, there have been few attempts to raise the Amarone and Valpolicella grape varieties outside of Italy.

Bardolino bears a marked resemblance to Valipolicella, which is not surprising as it is made from the same grapes. However, it tends to be somewhat lighter in body. On the other end of the weight spectrum is Amarone, also made from Corvina, Rondinella, and Molinara, but it is a big, full bodied wine, rich and velvety. The grapes are dried on bamboo racks for several months before undergoing fermentation. The dehydration concentrates the flavors and makes for a wine high in alcohol.

Like Pinot Grigio and Pinot Bianco from the nothernmost regions,

Soave is a popular dry white wine and is a blend of Garganega and Trebbiano grapes. The best Soaves come from the Classico area. Clean, crisp flavors, unmuddied by the ubiquitous winemaking techniques of oak flavoring and malolactic manipulation, result in a wine that is bright, pleasant, and especially delightful with seafood. Though these wines are rarely spectacular, the price is right, generally under $10 a bottle.

Southern Italian Wines

The south grows literally hundreds of different grapes, many brought to the area by the ancient Greeks, in the sixth and seventh centuries BC. The following are some of the most prominent red grapes, although the area produces many notable white wines as well. In Sicily, Planeta, Morgante, and Regaleali are prominent producers of wines made from the ancient Nero D'Avola grape. In Sardinia, Sella & Mosca and Argiolas make the red wine Cannonau, and in Calabria, the red wines Gaglioppo and Ciro are produced by Librandi. Basilicata grows Aglianico, one of southern Italy's finest red wines. In Apulia, the heel of the boot, Taurino and Botromagno produce Negro-amaro and Primitivo, which is related to American Zinfandel. In Campania, the red Taurasi, made from the Aglianico grape, is called "the Barolo of the south" because of its ability to age. Mastroberardino, Feudi di San Gregorio, and Villa Matilda are notable producers in the region. Most of these wineries produce wines that range from $10 to $12 all the way up to $50 a bottle and above. But at any price point, you'll taste remarkable wines, new to us in the United States but ancient in origin.

The Wines of Spain

Sherry

Sherry is one of the world's great fortified wines and comes from around the town of Jerez de la Frontera in southeastern Spain. The principal grape variety in Sherry is Palomino, plus small amounts of

Moscatel and Pedro Ximenez. Aguardiente, a colorless grape spirit similar to brandy, is added to the wine to raise the alcohol level to between 15 and 22 percent.

The two styles of Sherry are Fino and Oloroso. The Finos are pale in color, dry, with alcohol levels around 15 percent and with a bouquet of almonds. The Olorosos are higher in alcohol, rich and nutty in flavor, and amber to deep brown in color. They are usually dry. When Olorosos are sweet, they are called cream Sherries.

Rioja

The red wines from the Rioja region in northern Spain are made primarily of the Tempranillo grape with Grenache, Carignan, and Graciano also allowed into the blend. The wines are made in a Bordeaux style. Formerly the wines were heavily oaked; however, today they are made with the international market in mind.

Ribera del Duero

Some of Spain's most exciting wines are being made in this region several hundred miles north of Madrid. Again Tempranillo is the main grape varietal but also the Bordeaux varietals Cabernet Sauvignon, Malbec, and Merlot, along with Grenache are often part of the wine.

Pesquera is probably the best known wine producer from the region. The wines are outstanding in good vintages, and considering their quality, are reasonably priced at around $25 a bottle. They are made from 100 percent Tempranillo.

Penedes

South of Barcelona is the Penedes region where the primary producer is the house of Torres. The reds are blends of Tempranillo, Grenache, Carignan, and the Bordeaux varietals, Cabernet Sauvignon and Merlot. Torres' Gran Coronas is 100 percent Cabernet Sauvignon and perhaps the best red wine of the region.

Most of the production of the area is devoted to the *cavas* or Spanish sparkling wines, which use the grape varieties Parellada, Macabeo, and Xarel-lo and some Chardonnay. (Now when someone asks what's in that glass of Freixenet you're drinking you know what to say.)

Wines of Portugal

The wine from Portugal that most people have heard of, if not actually tasted, is Port, which takes it name, not from the country, but from the town of Oporto, from where it was shipped to England in the late 1600s. A fortified wine, like sherry, it usually has an alcohol content of 18 to 20 percent. The five primary grape varieties that make up Port are Tinta Barroca, Tinta Cao, Tempranillo, Touriga Francesa, and Touriga Nacional. With the exception of Tempranillo, you're not likely to encounter these varietals anywhere else, except on a wine trivia quiz. Top producers are Graham, Fonseca, Dow, and Quinta da Noval.

12

Wine and Health

Many different medical sources have substantiated that the consumption of wine in moderate amounts has definite health benefits that may help you to live a longer and healthier life. A healthier life is most likely a more productive life. In short, the less time you are ill, the more time you can spend earning money, whether you are employed by others, self-employed, in a fast-track career, or actively managing your investments. It may be argued that drinking wine is like putting money in your pocket because of its many beneficial effects.

The health benefits of wine were first brought to the attention of the American public more than ten years ago when the CBS television program, *60 Minutes*, broadcast a segment titled the "French Paradox." Harry Reasoner, the show's journalist, reported a phenomenon in France that seemed to defy the medical profession's ideas about health and diet. It seemed that the French, well-known consumers of rich foods covered with sauces loaded with fat and cheeses filled with calories, foods known to contribute to both high cholesterol and heart problems, had, in fact, a rate of heart disease much lower than many countries whose diets were much lower in heart-threatening foods. This was the paradox. Medical evidence suggested that the French should have been having heart attacks right and left, when in fact they were not. The answer to this seeming riddle was that the French consumed wine, which mitigated many of the dangerous effects of their high-fat diet. In fact, large, reliable studies show that moderate consumption of wine reduces the risk of cardiovascular disease by lowering LDL cholesterol and inhibiting the clotting of blood platelets that can lead to stroke.

New studies also point to other diverse benefits that are less well known, such as reduced risk of kidney stones; lower incidence of dementia and Alzheimer's disease; reduced risk for age-related macular degeneration, the leading cause of blindness for those over sixty-five; reduced risk for adult-onset diabetes; beneficial effects on bone-mineral density; and protection against digestive disorders caused by salmonella, shigella, and *E. coli* bacteria.

The largest and most important studies conclude that moderate consumption of wine and other alcoholic beverages protect people from coronary heart disease and stroke, the two leading causes of death throughout the developed world. The studies most often quoted are the Nurses' Health Study, the Framingham Study, the report by Thun, et al., from an American Cancer Society study, and the Copenhagen Heart Study.

Since we are partial to wine, we need to point out that these studies measure the benefit of alcohol consumption in general, not specifically wine, although wine and especially red wine may have added benefits. Wine is also traditionally consumed in the context of a meal and most easily lends itself to regular, moderate consumption, which has the utmost importance in all studies while excessive or inappropriate consumption clearly leads to adverse effects.

The Copenhagen Heart Study followed thirteen thousand men and women for more than ten years, and drinkers who averaged one to six drinks per week had 35 percent lower death rates than nondrinkers. Heavy drinkers had higher death rates, but nondrinkers had a much higher risk of death due to increased cardiovascular disease.

The Nurses' Health Study found that folate was associated with less coronary heart disease and that protection was much greater among drinkers than among abstainers. The risk of coronary heart disease was reduced by nearly 80 percent among women consuming fifteen grams of ethanol per day, ethanol being that form of alcohol in consummable beverages. Similarly, the Lyon Diet Heart Study found that moderate wine drinkers had higher blood levels of vitamin E than those who were ingesting it from other sources. In other words, wine consumption may enhance folate and vitamin E in the diet, both of which contribute to coronary health.

However, the Nurses' Health Study, among others, showed an alarming increase in breast cancer in moderate drinkers, although only excessive consumption seems to be responsible for other cancers, including upper digestive cancers and liver cancer. The Framingham Study that followed five thousand women for twenty-five to forty-five years, recently reported no increased risk of breast cancer for light- to moderate-drinking women who consumed either beer, wine, or spirits. Other recent research shows that adequate folate in the diet protects against this risk.

Finally, Thun, et al., and an American Cancer Society study that is following almost five hundred thousand people in the United States recently reported that men and women who consumed one to two drinks per day had death rates from any cause that were 21 percent lower than nondrinkers. So the research indicates that we should be focusing our efforts to reduce heavy, irresponsible drinking, not moderate use, which is clearly part of a healthy lifestyle.

While the benefits of drinking wine are many, an important caveat is that *these benefits apply to the moderate consumption of wine, from one to three five-ounce glasses of wine a day.* A 750-ml bottle of wine has approximately five glasses of wine in it. Once past the three-glass quota, the health benefits rapidly disappear. This is definitely a case where more is certainly not better!

Though the wine industry is happy to trumpet the beneficial findings of the "French Paradox," it rarely mentions that the French have one of the highest rates of cirrhosis of the liver in the world, a disease that is ultimately fatal as well as an extremely unpleasant way to die.

On another level, even short-term excessive use of wine or alcohol can have serious, even fatal consequences when combined with driving a motor vehicle. Even if an accident does not result, the financial consequences of driving drunk can be severe.

Over the last twenty years, efforts by groups like Mothers Against Drunk Driving (MADD) have led the courts and state legislatures to view drunk driving in ever harsher terms. The allowable blood alcohol level has steadily been lowered while fines and penalties have increased. In some states, a conviction for "driving while under the influence," commonly known as a DUI, means jail time as well as a substantial fine, mandatory classes in driving safety, and in some instances, loss of the driving privilege for six months to a year. In New York City, police are allowed to impound the car of a driver arrested for the first time for a DUI, even before a conviction. A first-time conviction in California will cost the individual thousands of dollars in fines, driving class costs, and greatly increased insurance rates.

If the insurance companies had their way, insurance would be denied to people convicted of drunk driving because the risk is too high. Fortunately for the rest of us, they are required by the states to do so. As compensation for the increased risk, they are allowed to charge three to five times the normal rate. In California, a person who is convicted of drunk driving becomes an assigned risk and remains so for seven years until the conviction is expunged from the record. That means seven years of astronomical insurance rates.

The cost for a California DUI will easily add up to over $10,000, not including lawyers' fees. In other words, instead of driving home from a party or a bar, a person who is arrested for driving while drunk, could have paid for five hundred $20 taxi cab rides. Nor would he or she have to spend time in court, in jail, or in class.

If you are not certain that you are within the legal blood alcohol limits, take a taxi. You'll still have $9,980 left, and no one will have been put at risk. It may possibly be the best investment you've ever made.

13

Past, Present, and Future

Cheapskating requires a lot more skill now than it did a few decades ago. As late as 1960, many Americans who lived in European enclaves, in cities, and especially on farms were making wines mostly for their own use and selling what they didn't need to their neighbors. You brought your jug to the barrel, paid your dollar, visited with the wine-maker, and drove home with your wine. Of course the wine wasn't usually very good.

Other Americans, if they drank wine at all, were buying jug wines made by a few giant wineries that had survived Prohibition, like Gallo, Sebastiani, Italian Swiss Colony, Krug, and Almaden. You could buy these wines cheaply at the grocery story and usually they were compe-tent but rarely exciting. With a few exceptions, most of the grapes that went into these wines were hardy varieties that were planted during Prohibition because they could survive travel across the country to people who were making wine for their own use. During the thirteen years of Prohibition, the law permitted only two legal uses for wine. You could make wine for your own personal consumption, or a vintner could make and sell it to the church for sacramental use.

Americans had their first experience with premium wine when they went to Europe as soldiers during World War II. There they drank lo-cally made wines from particular grape varieties that had survived in one place for hundreds of years. Americans also learned that Euro-peans drank wines with meals. In the United States, Prohibition had emphasized intoxication, so most Americans drank alcohol in recreational situations, in bars, at night clubs, and at parties.

Europeans, however, treated wine as a food and took the same pride in the wine they served as they did in the foods they cooked, sharing them with everyone at the dinner table, including the children. Wine enhanced food and aided digestion. Never did Europeans drink it for its intoxicating properties, just as most people do not eat in order to grow fat. Both wine and food were part of a local cultural tradition that had been handed down from parents to children for hundreds of years. Tuscans treasured the special foods and wines of their region, as did the Sicilians who treasured theirs, as did the Burgundians who treasured theirs.

When American soldiers returned to their homes in the United States, many of them searched for the wines they had tasted in Europe. As late as the 1960s, you could buy a first growth Bordeaux in the United States for as little as $9 or $10. Accounting for inflation, that amount might be about $30 now, which even the most rigorous cheapskate would be delighted to pay. But today, a first growth Bordeaux sells for between $250 and $500 a bottle, a painful price for even a latent cheapskate.

The next time that Americans invaded Europe was in the 1960s. The postwar boom was still booming, and Americans had enough extra money in their pockets to visit "Europe on $5 a day," the name of the travel guide whose most recent revision is *Europe from $50 a Day*. From $50 to what, we can only imagine. In the sixties, Europe was still recovering from World War II, and even students could easily afford to travel there. Once again, they had the European wine experience, enjoying enchanting, hand-crafted wines at every meal. But this time when they returned home, not only did they look for European wine in their neighborhood markets, but in California at least, a few of them jumped into the wine business, which had always been an important part of the economy ever since the good fathers first arrived to establish missions and civilize that wild state, a task they never quite finished.

Those who became winemakers began their quest to create the perfect Pinot Noir, the most elegant Cabernet Sauvignon, or the most scintillating Chardonnay, and those who went home to other jobs in other parts of the country began to create a sizable market for these better domestic wines. In the 1970s, most California vintners were still bottling wine in 1.5-liter jugs with screw tops, but they were paying more attention to grape varieties and began to make some fairly good Chardonnay and Cabernet Sauvignon.

Just as important as improved quality, the wines were truly dry table wines, meant to be consumed with meals. At the same time, of course, Americans were still drinking sweet recreational wines with added fruit flavors such as lemon, apple, or ginger, which were hardly wines at all, like Gallo's Thunderbird. Life was still easy for cheapskates. Both good domestic and imported wines were very reasonably priced, well within their comfort zone.

A lot of things changed, however, during the 1980s, including the price of wine, and those changes have persisted throughout the 1990s and into the new millennium. Americans have been getting older and a lot more health conscious, so they have been drinking less. Drunk driving laws have been popping up around the country and are being more strictly enforced, another reason to drink less. And finally, the rich have been getting richer, and prosperity has been trickling down effectively enough so that many people can pay a lot more for anything, including wine. Americans decided that if they must drink less, they would drink better, but they often confused higher prices with higher quality. So the race was on. A high score for a first growth Bordeaux or a small production California Cabernet could create a frenzy among people who could and would pay anything to have that wine on their tables, not a good setup for cheapskates.

While prices have increased, beyond reason many would argue, quality has improved enormously throughout all wine-producing countries. In California, viticulturists learned from the Europeans to evaluate which grape varieties would produce the best fruit in particular areas. They isolated those vineyards that produced superior fruit and put the vineyard names on the labels, as Europeans had always done. Vintners backed away from mass-produced wines and experimented with different winemaking techniques that preserved and enhanced the distinctiveness of different grapes from different areas.

Robert Mondavi argued that the French had become arrogant and sloppy, so they too have taken a closer look at farming techniques and winemaking practices. The Italians who had flooded the world with a few cheap, mass-produced wines were content to sell most of their wines in their own neighborhoods. In some cases, they were making wines the same way the Romans did with the same results, which by today's standards would be atrocious. In the last twenty years, they have modernized their vineyards and winemaking techniques and are producing some astounding world-class wines. The New Zealanders, who have a very young wine industry, are now making wonderful white wines, and the Australians are champions with Syrah. South Africa is also an emerging force in the wine world as is Latin America. The eastern bloc countries such as Hungary are some of the oldest and newest wine producers in the world.

In other words, life has become infinitely more complicated for cheapskates. The prices of many wines have soared, but infinitely more choices have appeared on shelves, many of which bring true joy to a cheapskate's heart, especially now that we all know what the best choices are.

14

Cheapskate Rules and Regulations

- Paying more for a wine won't make it taste better.
- Just because Robert Parker gave a wine a 95, doesn't mean you'll like it.
- A wine's value has nothing to do with whether or not you like it, but if the *Wine Spectator* or the *Wine Advocate* likes a wine, they can often affect its price.
- Wine reacts to the laws of supply and demand just like stamps or gold coins.
- There are very few truths or absolutes when it comes to wine but no shortage of opinions.
- The fruit flavors in a bottle of wine never increase with age—just the opposite.
- If a wine tastes really good now, drink it. Its chances of getting better are not as good as its chances of getting worse.
- If a wine is short on flavor, the winery will generally describe it as elegant or possessing finesse.
- Wines that are high in acid and taste somewhat tart are often described as "food wines" for good reason. They really do complement food much better than low acid wines. These wines generally do poorly in wine competitions.
- Those big, buttery, vanilla-flavored Chardonnays that taste like a

butterscotch sundae, are best enjoyed by themselves, perhaps as an aperitif before a meal.

- Remember: You don't drink gold medals or high scores.
- A good pairing of food and wine will enhance both.
- A bad combination of food and wine will diminish both.
- The right food with the right wine is heavenly.
- Always eat a little something, like bread, before drinking wine. It will make the wine taste better.
- Wines with noticeable tannins will taste better if you serve cheese with them. The proteins in the cheese soften the effect of the tannins in your mouth.
- The only thing more gauche than telling your guests that the wine you are serving received a score of 97 is telling them how much you paid for it.
- One of the benchmarks of a great wine is that guests at the dinner table will suddenly change the topic of conversation to appreciative exclamations, even those who rarely drink wine, since you don't need an educated palate or a lot of experience to recognize and appreciate a great wine.
- A great wine is the result of a simple process: Great fruit comes from a great vineyard in a great year and is then transformed into great wine by a great winemaker.
- Very few wines are great. Most people will never taste a great wine. Those who do are fortunate indeed.
- If the wine is to be the star of the dinner, cast the food in a supporting role.
- Good dinner companions make a good wine taste better. Don't pour your favorite wine when you know you will be sharing it with guests you wish were dining elsewhere.
- Wine snobs can't help their wine snobbery, nor can you help them, so don't even try. Not even professional counseling does any good. They live in a deterministic world with their DNA packet cursed with the dreaded Wine Snob gene.
- Under no circumstances should you ever consider putting a phony price tag on a bottle of wine intended as a gift, unless you are sure you won't get caught.

Glossary

Auslese: German white wine whose grapes possess a high degree of ripeness at the time of harvest. The grapes are often affected by *botrytis* (see below). In the German QMP (Qualitatswein Mit Pradikat or "Quality Wine With Distinction") classification, Auslese falls between Spatlese and Beerenauslese.

Balance: The relationship between the components in wine, especially acids, tannins, and fruit flavors, which should be in harmony, without any single element dominating the others.

Barrel fermentation: The labor-intensive process by which wine is fermented in smaller barrels instead of tanks and consequently exhibits different flavors imparted by the wood.

Beerenauslese: German white wine made from individually selected overripe grapes affected by *botrytis* (see below). Very rich and concentrated wine.

Bordeaux Classification: Originally drawn up in 1855, the classification of 61 Châteaux from the Medoc and Graves into five groups used the simple expedient of assigning a Château to a particular class based on how much its wine cost. The four most expensive wines were accorded First Growth status. The remaining 57 Châteaux were accordingly assigned Second, Third, Fourth, or Fifth Growth status, based on their cost. The only change in the following 150 years has been the elevation of Mouton-Rothschild from Second to First Growth status in 1973. The wines of Barsac and Sauternes were also classified in 1855 into First and Second Growths, with Ch. D'Yquem given the unique designation, First Great Growth. In 1955 the Châteaux of St. Emilion were classified, with Ch. Ausone and Ch. Cheval-Blanc given First Growth standing. The wines of Pomerol have never been classified, though Ch. Petrus is thought of as a First Growth.

Botrytis: A fungus that develops in the presence of excess humidity and shrivels the grapes, a condition sometimes called "noble rot" because it intensifies the flavors of the grapes, raises the sugars, and renders the fruit suitable for dessert wines.

Bouquet: The various aromas that emanate from a wine.

Brettanomyces: A yeast that reacts with amino acids in wine and produces an unpleasant taste and smell.

Brix: A scale that measures soluble solids, especially the sugar in grape juice, and helps to indicate when wine grapes should be picked.

Carbonic maceration: Fermentation in the interior of whole uncrushed grapes, which are producing carbon dioxide, in the presence of fermenting juice.

Cold fermentation: Fermenting juice for white wine at lower temperatures, which create a lighter wine.

Corkage: The fee that a restaurant charges for serving a wine that a patron brings to the restaurant.

Crush: Breaking the grape skins to release the juice and separating stems and leaves from the juice and other grape solids.

Dry farming: Farming without irrigation so that vines have access to minimal moisture and produce more intensely flavored fruit.

Fermentation: The natural chemical process that produces wine when sugar is converted to alcohol and carbon dioxide. Natural airborne yeast or added yeast is the catalyst.

Fifth Growth or *Cinquième Cru*: Fifth rank of the Bordeaux Classification.

Filtration: Removing any solids from wine before bottling.

Fining: Using certain substances, such as carbon, charcoal, casein, egg whites, or gelatin, that absorb or coagulate suspended particles in the wine and clarify the wine as they sink to the bottom of the tank.

Finish: The impression a wine leaves in the mouth after it is swallowed, a longer, distinctive finish is the ideal.

First Growth or *Premier Cru*: The highest of five ranks established by law in 1855 to classify the red wines of Bordeaux.

Fortified: The addition of brandy or some other spirit to add flavor and increase the alcohol content of a wine such as Port, Sherry, Madiera, or Marsala, originally a method for preserving certain wines.

Fourth Growth or *Quatrième Cru*: Fourth rank in the Bordeaux Classification.

Hand-made wines: Wines made by small wineries without elaborate equipment that instead are made by older labor-intensive methods.

Kabinett: The first harvested and generally the lightest and least ripe of the German white wines in the QMP classification. Following the Kabinett level wines in ascending order of ripeness are the Spätlese, Auslese, Beerenauslese, and Trokenbeerenauslese.

Lees: The sediment that sinks to the bottom of the tank after fermentation, consisting mainly of grape particles and dead yeast cells. The wine is then drained or racked into another tank or barrels.

Malolactic fermentation: A secondary fermentation that occurs after the alcoholic fermentation and converts harsh malic acid into softer lactic acid. This second fermentation also produces diacetyl, which smells like warm butter, especially apparent in California Chardonnay.

Methode Champenoise: Producing sparkling wine by adding sugar and yeast to wine and quickly bottling and corking it so that a second fermentation takes place in the bottle, creating additional alcohol and trapped carbon dioxide gas, or bubbles, in the wine.

Oak: The wood most often preferred for barrels in which wine is stored and aged. Winemakers choose barrels carefully because the wood imparts particular flavors and tannins to the wines.

pH: The measure of acidity/alkalinity in wine that represents the intensity of the acid, whereas total acidity, another common measure of acid, measures the volume of acid in the wine.

Pressing: Follows crushing and separates the juice from the skins and pips by squeezing the grapes before fermentation for white wines and after fermentation for red wines.

Racking: Draining a wine off the lees at the bottom of the tank or barrel into another container, an activity that occurs several times during the winemaking process.

Residual sugar: Unfermented sugar that remains in a wine at a barely perceptible level in some dry wines or obviously in sweet wines.

Second Growth or *Deuxième Cru*: Second rank of the Bordeaux Classification.

Skin contact: Allowing the unfermented juice destined to become white wine to remain in contact with the skins and seeds for a short period before fermentation to intensify flavors.

Spätlese: German white wine designation literally meaning "late harvest." The grapes are picked at least one week after the grapes for the Kabinett level wines, and possess greater ripeness and higher sugar levels. Made in both a dry (Trocken) and a sweet style.

Sur lees: Wine that remains on the lees without racking or filtration before bottling.

Tannins: Molecules that leach into the juice and wine from the skins, seeds, and stems of grapes and from wood barrels, especially new ones; they have harsh, bitter flavors in certain young red wines but also have antioxidant properties that allow red wines to age. As time goes on, the tannin molecules link up and fall out of solution, leaving an older wine smooth and mellow.

Terroir: A French term for the total environment in which the vine develops, especially the soil, slope, drainage, and climate.

Third Growth or *Troisième Cru*: Third rank of Bordeaux Classification.

Trockenbeerenauslese: Ripest and richest of the German wines in the QMP classification. Made from shriveled grapes affected by *botrytis* or noble rot. Extremely concentrated, unctuous wines.

Varietal: The particular grape variety from which a wine is made, for example, Cabernet Sauvignon, Chardonnay, or Syrah.

Vertical tasting: Comparing the wines of a particular winery from consecutive years, whereas a horizontal tasting would be comparing the wines from multiple wineries made in the same year.

Vinify: Commonly used in Europe to indicate the process of turning grapes into wine.

Viticulture: The process of farming grape vines.

Recommended Books

Anderson, Burton. *The Wine Atlas of Italy and Traveler's Guide to the Vineyards*. London: Mitchell Beazley, 1997.

Broadbent, Michael. *The Simon & Schuster Pocket Guide to Wine Tasting*. New York: Fireside/Simon and Schuster, 1988.

Broadbent, Michael. *The New Great Vintage Wine Book*. New York: Alfred A. Knopf, 1991.

Duijker, Hubrecht. *The Wine Atlas of Spain*. New York: Antique Collectors Club, 1997.

Halliday, James. *The Wine Atlas of California*. New York: Viking, 1993.

Halliday, James. *The Wine Atlas of Australia and New Zealand*. San Francisco: The Wine Appreciation Guild, 2000.

Johnson, Hugh. *The World Atlas of Wine*. New York: Simon and Schuster, 1985.

Parker, Robert M. *Bordeaux*. New York: Simon and Schuster, 1998.

Robinson, Jancis. *The Oxford Companion to Wine*. Oxford: Oxford University Press, 1999.

Index

Abruzzo, 69–70
Absentee bidding, 157–58
Acidity, 106–7
Acker Merral and Condit, 32, 130, 160
Aging of wines, 101–7, 111–12
Alsace, 170
   Gewürtztraminers, 66
   Pinot Blancs, 64
Amarone, 135, 175
Ambrosia, 36
Appraisals, 142–43, 144
Asti Spumante, 172–73
Auctions, 143–47, 151–60. *See also*
     Bidding, at auctions
   catalogs, 151–54
   charity, 149–50
   houses, 160
   reserves, 146, 158–59
   who benefits from, 159
Australia
   Cabernet Sauvignons, 52–53
   Chardonnays, 47
   Syrahs, 61
   wineries, 86

Barbaresco, 134–35, 171–72
Bars, wine, 71–72
Beaujolais, 169
Beaulieu Vineyards, 78–79
Beerenausleses, 138–40
Bel-Air: Twenty Twenty International
   Wine Merchants, 28–29, 131

Beltramo's Fine Wines and Spirits, 31,
   132
Belvedere Winery, 84
Bidding, at auctions, 154–55
   absentee, 157–58
   on mixed lots, 156–57
   on multiple lots, 155–56
Bogle Winery, 14, 82–83
Bonny Doon Vineyard, 80–82
Books, 7, 194
Bordeaux, 168
   Cabernet Sauvignons, 50–51, 168
   classification, 189–90
   collecting, 117–18, 122–28, 132
   futures, 127–28, 129–32
   Merlots, 53–54, 168
Brettanomyces, 163, 190
Brown Derby International Wine
   Center, 31, 130–31
Brunello di Montalcino, 67, 68, 174
Burgundy, 132–34, 168–69
   Chardonnays, 46
   Pinot Noirs, 56–57, 168
Butterfield and Butterfield, 160
Buying wines. *See* Purchasing wines

Cabernet Sauvignon, 49–53, 168
   best value, 15, 51–53
   food pairings with, 92, 93
   futures, 128–29
California
   Cabernet Sauvignons, 50, 51–52,
     128–29

California (*cont.*)
  Chardonnays, 46–47
  Chenin Blancs, 66
  futures, 128–29
  Gewürztraminers, 66
  Merlots, 54
  Pinot Noirs, 57, 58
  Rieslings, 65
  Sangiovese, 68–69
  Sauvignon Blancs, 62–63
  sparkling wines, 49
  Syrahs, 61–62
  wineries, 77–85
  Zinfandels, 55, 56
California Wine Club, 37
Cardiovascular health, 179–81
Catalogs, auction, 151–54
Celebrations Wine Club, 34–35
Champagne, 47–48, 171
  chilling quickly, 88–89
Chardonnay, 14, 45–47, 92, 171
Charitable giving, of wines, 149–50
Château Souverain, 79
Chenin Blanc, 66–67, 170
Chianti, 67–68, 134–35, 173–74
Chilling wines, 88–89
Classes, wine, 74
Clubs
  price, members-only, 18–19
  wine-of-the-month, 33–38, 73–74
  winery, 38–39
  wine tasting, 72–73
Collecting wines, 101–40
  Bordeaux, 117–18, 122–29, 132
  Burgundy, 132–34
  Cabernet Sauvignons, 128–29
  futures, 127–32
  German wines, 138–40
  insurance, 111, 141–43
  as investment, 120–21
  Italian wines, 134–35
  Parker and, 123–25
  Ports, 135–36
  price escalation and, 119–20
  reasons for, 107–9, 116–17
  from the Rhône Valley, 140
  risks of, 109–12
  Sauternes, 137
  storage, 112–15
  track record and, 119
Columbia Crest Winery, 85
Competitions, 7–12
  how they work, 7–10
  number scores, 11–12

Copycat wines, 10, 110–11
Corks, 96–97
Cost Plus, 29
Counterfeit wines, 110–11

D & M Wine and Liquor, 29
Decanting wine, 95–96
Decantor, 127
Dee Vine Wines, 28
Dinners, wine, 73
Discounters (discount stores), 19
Dolcetto, 172
Donating wines, 149–50
Drunk driving, 181–82
Dry Creek Valley, 55, 84

Estancia Winery, 84–85
eVineyard.com, 33

Fetzer Vineyards, 15, 16, 77
Fino, 177
Food, pairing wine with, 90–94, 164–65
Food section, of newspapers, 2
France. *See also specific regions*
  Chenin Blancs, 66
  Sauvignon Blancs, 63
  wineries, 85–86
  wines of, 168–71
"French Paradox," 179, 181
Futures, 127–32

Georges Duboeuf, 85–86
Germany
  collecting wines from, 138–40
  Rieslings, 64–65
Gewürztraminer, 16, 65–66, 170
Glasses, wine, 94–95
Glossary of terms, 189–93
Gold Medal Wine Club, 36
Grape varietals, 45–70, 167. *See also specific varietals*
Grenache, 60

Health benefits of wine, 179–82
Hess Winery, 83–84
History, 183–86
House wines, at restaurants, 166

Inexpensive wines, top value, 13–16
Information sources, 2–7
  for collecting wines, 123–27
Insurance, for wines, 111, 141–43
Investment, wine as, 120–21
Italy

collecting wines from, 134–35
Sangiovese, 67–68
southern wines, 69–70, 176
wines of, 171–76

Jerez de la Frontera, 176–77

K and L Wine Merchants, 23–24, 131
Kermit Lynch, Wine Merchant, 11–12,
    24–26, 60, 61, 170

Labels, wine, 153–54
Languedoc-Roussillon, Syrahs, 60–61
Lindemans Winery, 86
Lockwood Winery, 78
Loire Valley, 63, 170

MacArthur Liquors, 30, 129, 130
Magazines. *See* Publications
Merchants. *See* Retailers
Meridian Vineyards, 14, 79–80
Merlot, 14, 53–55, 168
Meunier, 47, 171
Mixed lots, 156–57
Money-saving tips
    inexpensive wines, top value, 13–16
    for restaurants, 164–66
Multiple lots, 155–56
Muscadet, 170

Napa Valley. *See* California
Nebbiolo, 172
Newsletters, from wine merchants, 3
Newspapers, as information source, 2
New Zealand, Sauvignon Blancs, 63–64
Northern Rhône Valley, 59, 140, 169–70

Oak barrels, 9, 46, 192
Oldfield Brokerage Corporation, 141–42
Oloroso, 177
Oregon
    Pinot Noirs, 57, 58–59
    Rieslings, 65
Oregon Pinot Noir Club, 37
Oregon Wine Club, 37
Oxford Companion to Wine, 7

Pacific Northwest. *See also* Oregon;
    Washington State
    Chardonnays, 47
Palomino, 176–77
Parker, Robert, 4–5, 10, 30, 123–25, 126
Passport Wine Club, 38
Penedes, 177–78

Pesquera, 177
Phillips Auctioneers, 160
Piedmont, 135, 171–73
Pinot Blanc, 64, 170
Pinot Gris, 64, 170
Pinot Noir, 56–59, 64, 168, 171
    best value, 14–15, 58–59
    food pairings with, 92, 93
Ports, 178
    vintage, 135–36
Portugal, wines of, 178
Pouilly-Fume, 170
Prearrivals, 132
Premier Cru, 26–27, 131
Price clubs, 18–19
Price escalation, 119–20
Private parties, 39–40
Private Preserve, 99
Publications, 3–7, 43, 106–7
    collecting wines and, 123–27
Purchasing wines, 13–40. *See also*
    Retailers
    clubs, 33–39
    discount stores, 19
    inexpensive wines, top value, 13–16
    price clubs, 18–19
    private parties, 39–40
    supermarkets, 16–18

Rabbit Ridge, 80
Red wines. *See also specific grape vari-*
    etals
    collecting, 115–16
    food pairing with, 91–92
    house, at restaurants, 166
    tannins and acids in, 104–7
    temperature, 87, 89
Restaurants, 161–66
    bargains in, 164–66
    bringing your own wine, 161–62
    house wines, 166
    returning wines, 162–64
Retailers, 19–33
    East Coast, 30, 130
    Midwest, 31, 130–31
    newsletters, 3
    selling wines to, 148
    West Coast, 21–29, 131–32
    wine futures and, 129–32
Rhône Valley, 169–70
    collecting wines from, 140
    Syrahs, 59, 60
Ribera del Duero, 177
Riedel wine glasses, 94–95

Rioja, 15, 177
Riseling, 64–65, 170
Rosemount Winery, 15, 86

Sam's Wine and Spirits, 31, 131
Sancerre, 170
Sangiovese, 67–69, 173
Sauternes, 137, 171
Sauvignon Blanc, 62–64, 92, 170, 171
Saving opened wine, 97–100
Scams, 109–10
Sediment, 24–25, 95–96
Selling wines, 143–49. *See also* Auctions
   on commission, 149
   privately, 149
   to retailers, 148
Serving wine, 87–100
   corks, 96–97
   decanting, 95–96
   pairing with food, 90–94
   saving opened wine, 97–100
   temperature, 87–89
   wine glasses, 94–95
Sherry, 176–77
Sherry-Lehmann, 32, 160
Shipping wines, 19–21, 39
Soave, 175–76
Sonoma Valley. *See* California
Sotheby's, 160
South America, Chardonnay, 47
Southern Italian wines, 69–70, 176
Southern Rhône Valley, 59, 60, 140,
   169–70
Spain, wines of, 49, 176–78
Sparkling wines, 15, 48–49, 88
Storage (storing wines), 112–15
Supermarket deals, 16–18
Syrah, 14, 15, 59–62, 92

Tannins, 104–6, 193
Tastings, 72–73
Tax deductions, for wines, 149–50
Temperature, of wine, 87–89
   storage and, 113–14
Track record of wine, 119, 124–25
Trader Joe's, 19
Trockenbeerenausleses, 138–40
Tuscany, 67–68, 134–35, 173–75

Vacu-Vin, 99
Valpolicella, 175
Varietals. *See* Grape varietals

Veneto, 135, 175–76
Vernaccia, 174–75
Vineyards. *See* Wine producers; *and
   specific vineyards*
Vintages, 41–70. *See also* Collecting
   wines
   aging of wines, 101–7, 117–18
   grape varietals, 45–70
   Ports, 135–36

Warming wines, 88–89
Washington State
   Cabernet Sauvignons, 52
   Chenin Blancs, 66, 67
   Merlots, 54–55
White wines. *See also specific grape vari-
   etals*
   chilling quickly, 88–89
   collecting, 115
   food pairing with, 91–92
   house, at restaurants, 166
   temperature, 87–88
Wide World of Wines, 32, 130
Wine Advocate, 4–6, 10, 11, 43, 123–25,
   126, 139
Wine auctions. *See* Auctions
Wine bars, 71–72
Wine cellars, 114–15
Wine classes, 74
Wine Club, 21–22, 131
Wine competitions. *See* Competitions
Wine Connection, 31
Wine dinners, 73
Wine Discount Center, 32
Wine Enthusiast, 6–7, 12, 126, 139
Wine futures, 127–32
Wine glasses, 94–95
Wine merchants. *See* Retailers
Wine-of-the-month clubs, 33–38, 73–74
Wine producers (wineries), 75–86
   American, 77–85
   Australian, 86
   French, 85–86
Wine publications. *See* Publications
Winery clubs, 38–39
Wine Spectator, 3–4, 11–12, 43–44, 126,
   139, 142–43, 148
Wine tastings, 72–73

Zachy's, 30, 130, 160
Zinfandel, 14, 55–56, 92